Remnants
Marisa Gary

Strongtower Media & Entertainment
PO Box 730653
Ormond Beach, FL 32173

Copyright © 2009 Marisa Gary.
Printed and bound in the United States of America.

All rights reserved. No part of this book may be reproduced or transmitted in any form or by any means, electronic or mechanical, including photocopying, recording, or by an information storage and retrieval system—except by a reviewer who may quote brief passages in a review to be printed in a magazine or newspaper— without permission in writing from the publisher.

ISBN: 978-0-578-01250-6

Scripture taken from the HOLY BIBLE, NEW INTERNATIONAL VERSION®. Copyright © 1973, 1978, 1984 International Bible Society. Used by permission of Zondervan. All rights reserved. The "NIV" and "New International Version" trademarks are registered in the United States Patent and Trademark Office by International Bible Society. Use of either trademark requires the permission of International Bible Society.

Scripture taken from The Message. Copyright 1993, 1994, 1995, 1996, 2000, 2001, 2002. Used by permission of Navpress Publishing Corp.

Scripture quotations marked "NCV" are taken from the New Century Version®. Copyright © 2005 by Thomas Nelson, Inc. Used by permission. All rights reserved.

Acknowledgements

I would like to thank the Lord for waiting patiently on me to come to Him.

To my children, Ashley, Justin and TJ; may you always find God in the simplest places - inside your heart.

To my husband, Robert; thank you for introducing me to our Lord. You are my best friend. Thank you for loving me through everything - even through my need to constantly sweep the floor. I love you.   Shmily.

Mom, you made me strong.
Dad, you made me smart.
Nana, you & Pop loved me no matter what I did.
Thank you. I couldn't have done this if you hadn't prepared me long ago.

Thank you, Tomoka Christian Church, where the pastors teach the Word of God as it is written, not as we want it to read.

Dana, Stephanie, Gigi and Sandy: I marvel at how blessed I am to have the most amazing women of God as my friends! Thank you for showing me how to be a friend and how to accept love from friends. I love each of you and I don't know what I would do without your laughter, your advice and your honesty.

Thanks to all of women on W@H. We may be scattered around the world, but our friendships are real. www.wahministry.com

Robin—I love you and I am so proud of how much you have accomplished!

Dedication

This book is dedicated to Richard Littleton.

On a cold night, eating fish sandwiches on a smelly dock, you convinced me that God would use your cancer to bring others to Christ. I was mad that this happened to you, but you considered it a gift; you said God chose you as an instrument for His work.

I started writing these devotions the very next day.

Foreword

And without faith it is impossible to please God, because anyone who comes to him must believe that he exists and that he rewards those who earnestly seek him.
(Hebrews 11:6NIV)

My story is anything but simple. I did not take the smooth, paved road on my journey to meet God. Instead of the straight road, took the winding, curving road riddled with danger signs, road blocks and construction zones. It took me 33 years to figure out what my son learned in nine years: God is the way, the truth and the life. (John 14:6)

Before the age of 30, I was divorced twice; I had declared bankruptcy, and was a single mother. I was at the bottom. Slowly but steadily I was climbing out of the pit I had single-handedly dug for myself.

Then, in 2004, I met a man who would change my life forever. He was a Christian and, while we were dating, he asked if I believed in God. Not even knowing what that meant, I said I did, figuring I could fake my way through it. I didn't even know what it really meant.

After we married, it took a long time for our family to start attending church. My husband had made the decision that we were going to find a good church. I remember him warning me before walking through the doors of the first church we were going to try that I might not like what I was about to experience. He said it was very different from what I was used to. "Cool," I thought, "that's just what I need." God had already softened my heart and was preparing me for what I was about to experience.

Then, I walked in the doors and saw......... nothing.

No alter,
No statutes,
No stations,
No pews,
No stained glass,
No tabernacle,
No crucified man hanging from the ceiling.
And I was thrilled.

Then a man stood up and stepped onto the "stage" area. He was dressed in jeans and an un-tucked shirt. He announced himself as the youth pastor who normally occupies a building behind the one we were in, but several times a year, he and his youth band led worship. "Lead worship?" I didn't know what that meant but I couldn't wait to find out.

Craig Portwood, the youth pastor, along with singers and a band stepped onto the stage. The lights dimmed, the screen started showing moving, bright colors and then....words! Wow.

What happened next should have made me run out the door. People were standing, clapping, holding their hands up in the air and praising God. What??? What was going on? I was mesmerized. For the first time in my life, I saw people worshipping God – and I wanted some.

This moment started a change in my life. I listened to the youth pastor's sermon and I thought to myself (as I still do to this day), "Gee, that doesn't just apply to kids; that applies to my life too."

We started attending this church regularly, and soon I heard the senior pastor, Joe Putting, say the one phrase that will stay with me the rest of my life. "Grace and Mercy." Grace is when God gives us what we don't deserve. Mercy is when God does not give us what we do deserve." Those were the words I needed to hear.

Over the next six months, I dove into the Word. I read, I studied, I learned, I asked, and I prayed. My life was changing. My kids' lives were changing. On April 5, 2006, my husband baptized our oldest daughter and then he baptized me. I felt my old self stay in the water and I've walked with Jesus ever since that day.

One year later, my husband baptized our youngest. At the age of 10, he has a passion for the Lord that most adults don't possess.

Every day that passes, I grow closer to God. He guides my every day, pushing my boundaries further from my comfort zone. My thoughts, which have become filled with my faith, were always solely my own. I never thought I would write them down and offer them out to others. Yet here I am, writing a foreword to my first book. Pastor Joe taught me that if I'm comfortable in my walk, I'm probably not where God wants me to be. It is not until we rely completely on God that we find ourselves where He wants us to be.

I am just about at that place now. Even so, I am sure that as soon as I am comfortable here, He'll move me again, ever pushing those boundaries further out.

What happens next? I don't know. I will continue to grow and to learn. I will strive to teach my children to always do what is right in the face of the Lord. I will continue to treat my husband as the other half of myself as the Bible says I should. I will love the Lord my God with all my heart, soul, mind and strength. I will boldly walk to the foot of the throne and offer my prayers as though they are already answered. I will keep my thoughts pure and my ways simple.

Your statutes are wonderful;
therefore I obey them.
The unfolding of your words
gives light; it gives
understanding to the simple.

Psalm 119:129-130 NIV

Palms of My Hands

I will not forget you. See, I have inscribed you on the palms of my hands. (Isaiah 49:15-16 NRSV)

Walking with Christ takes more than a decision. It is a life-long commitment to live according to scripture, to follow the path that Christ took. It is a progression that begins with a decision to dedicate our lives to our Maker, followed by an act of obedience, the baptism. For so many Christians, it ends there. Salvation is ensured, but it should not stop here. In fact, ending here is to miss the sweet reward of walking Christ's walk.

Living for Christ is something very different. Living each moment conscious of God's presence requires specific actions on our part. First, we must live beyond reproach. Our words, our deeds, our motives must remain pure and our hearts must belong to God. Even if we share our heart with our spouse or our children, we first belong to God. As Abraham offered up his only son to his Lord, we should live first for God, then for our family.

Once our words, deeds, motives and hearts belong to God, we take on a mark of sorts. It is not a physical mark as a tattoo, but a spiritual mark that is just as visible. It is a sign that we live for God. It is a mark most noticeable to those of the world who do not know God or the power he has on our lives. Wearing this mark for all to see shows our boldness in Christ and our humbleness that we are nothing without our God.

LORD, give me the strength to wear your mark in every part of my life. Give me the words to speak to those who know you not. Give me peace in my heart to accept what I cannot have because I have you.

Can others see your mark?

I Am What I Am

"But by the grace of God I am what I am, and his grace to me was not without effect" (1 Corinthians 15:10 NIV)

I spent many, many years thinking I needed to be better. I needed to be skinnier, prettier, smarter, more refined, and of course, healthier.

These are the things that everyone strives for, right?

I was not OK with who or what I was. I was "broken" and needed to get fixed. For a very long time, my illness was simply unacceptable to me. I told very few people I was sick at all, lest they not trust me to do something or think I was less of a person because of the overwhelming fatigue that I usually experience. I would push through the exhaustion to get a task completed, just so I could say that I did it.

I realize though, that I am what I am. That may sound too simplistic, but it is the truth. This is the way I was made, this is who I am. My illness, while it does not define me, it refines me; not like a shiny jewel, but like a worn, used jar of clay. I will never be a marathon runner, I will never compete in the Olympics, and I will never be a firefighter, police officer or doctor. I accept these limitations. I am a Christian and I follow my Lord wherever He leads me; that is enough for me.

Holy Lord, you made me, use me as I am for your will. I am here, I am ready and I am waiting to glorify you in any way you see fit.

Are you ready to let the Lord use you for His will?

Consider My Sighing

"Give ear to my words, O LORD, consider my sighing. Listen to my cry for help, my King and my God, for to you I pray. In the morning, O LORD, you hear my voice; in the morning I lay my requests before you and wait in expectation." (Psalm 5:1-3 NIV)

Have the pressures of the day ever been so great that getting out of bed almost seemed impossible? I know that there are days when the crushing weight of the world seems insurmountable. These are the days I know I cannot begin my day without going to God first.

Prayer is not like fast-food. We cannot "place an order" and expect that God will realize that we know better and do what we ask because we ask. No, instead, we lay it all before the throne, understanding that our prayers may or may not be answered in the fashion we requested. Only God knows what is best, and it is up to us to trust Him enough.

So, I let out my cry for help and wait in expectation; not for my will to be done, but for God's will to be done. Sometimes I just need to cry out to God and beg for understanding. Then I wait.......I wait for an answer.

LORD, please answer me. I wait for you in expectation, needing to hear your voice, needing to hear that you are helping me carry this burden. LORD, my entire life is in your hands. Help me walk the path that you have laid for me.

Can you cry out and wait for God to answer?

Life

After the sudden, and extremely unexpected death of a co-worker, I am reminded that we are not guaranteed a tomorrow. I thought about his children and how he had every intention of having dinner with his little girl that night. I think about the possibilities of words left unsaid, left for another day; apologies left un-given; forgiveness left un-granted. I've been riddled with the thought that those I care about most in this world may not even realize they are in the top 10.

Therefore, I've decided to do a few things. First, I have to start living like tomorrow may never come. I need to make sure I forgive and apologize and love and hug and all the things that I put off to tomorrow. Those closest to me need to know how much they mean to me...today.

Second, I need to put my pen to paper and write letters to my children. I know someone who did this a year or two ago and I loved the idea, but as my nature, I put it off for another day. I want the letters written this month, while the need, the urgency is still pulsing through me.

Third, I need to change my attitude. Can you imagine living your last day miserable because you spilled coffee on your favorite shirt, or because you fought with your wife over who was going to cook that night? What if you never made it home?? What good then is the fight over a dinner you will never eat? I think this is the hardest task of all to overcome, because as Americans, as humans, we are so used to living in the moment that we forget to look at the big picture and see that none of the day to day's doldrums matters.

So, if you're reading this, I challenge you to re-evaluate the things that are most important in your life. When was the last time you hugged your spouse; your kids; your dog? It's time to draw your line in the sand and take your everydays back. They belong to you. We only get one time around this life. We'll never get today back we never get a chance to do a day over, a moment over... Did you spend today the way you should have? Take the time to figure out how you would spend your last day; and spent it every day.

LORD, I live for you and in doing so, you allowed me to have a family, friends and a life that is worth living. I thank you for the time you give me to spend with those who mean the most to me.

Go tell your Top 10 that they're tops.

Walk on Water

"During the fourth watch of the night Jesus went out to them, walking on the lake. When the disciples saw him walking on the lake, they were terrified. "It's a ghost," they said, and cried out in fear. But Jesus immediately said to them: "Take courage! It is I. Don't be afraid." "Lord, if it's you," Peter replied, "tell me to come to you on the water." "Come," he said. Then Peter got down out of the boat, walked on the water and came toward Jesus. But when he saw the wind, he was afraid and, beginning to sink, cried out, "Lord, save me!" Immediately Jesus reached out his hand and caught him. "You of little faith," he said, "why did you doubt?" (Matthew 14:25-31 NIV)

Many people miss the whole point of this story. The focus is usually on the fact that Peter sank because he didn't have enough faith to trust in Jesus. The point is that in order to sink, first had to have walked on water. Peter did it; and he was the only one. No one else on that boat had the faith or the courage to stand up and say 'I trust you enough.'

I just returned from a mission trip in Montana. It was a manual labor trip. Groups baled hay, milked cows, built houses, repaired houses and painted decks. I was on the team that painted a 200' deck in four days.

On any given day throughout the year, there is no way I can do this kind of work, let alone for four days straight. I am not strong enough; my muscles tire far too easily for ten hour days like this. There were several of us who could never have accomplished this kind of task at home.

Why were we able to do it there? We trusted God. We gave Him our hurts and our illnesses for a week and He gave us the strength we needed to get the work done. It's pretty amazing; none of us were sore after all that work. God is good. When we trust in Him, when we are not afraid to put it all on the line for Him, He rewards us.

God, I trust you enough. Tell me to come and I will obey. I want you to work through me, allowing me to do things that others know can only be done through the grace of your hand.

Do you have the faith of Peter? Will you step out of the boat?

Strong Support

"For the eyes of the LORD move to and fro throughout the earth that He may strongly support those whose heart is completely His" (2 Chronicles 16:9 NIV)

We always like to have someone near us who 'has our back.' Sometimes it's a best friend, sometimes a sibling, or a spouse. These people care about us and do their best to make sure that we stay safe.
But isn't it amazing when God looks out for us, searching for those whose hearts are completely His? He is looking for us and wants to be near us because we took that step and decided to give our whole hearts to our King.

And what does He do when He finds us? He strongly supports us. God has our back! What a wonderful feeling. I know that God will be there for me because I have given my whole heart completely to Him. I never have to fear, and I never have to worry because God will always be right there beside me.

Lord, here I am! I give my whole self to you in the hope that you will support me. Mold me to do your will so that I may never be without you, not even for a moment.

How does God have your back?

Why Am I So Discouraged?

"Why am I discouraged? Why so sad? I will put my hope in God! I will praise him again – my Savior and my God." (Psalm 42:11 NLT)

I used to try to do it all by myself. I didn't need an invisible God to heal me or work through my issues. Yet every time I put that kind of pressure on myself, I would fail.

When we put our hope, trust and confidence in things of this world, we often find ourselves discouraged and sad. We'll find ourselves wondering why bad things happen to us. 'Why me' is uttered far too often.

Put your hope in God. He is the one who can turn your life around. He is the one we are called to put our trust, hope and confidence in. By giving up the burdens of this world, we are freed. We no longer have to be subject to the evils around us. We are freed from the confines of this world, we are free in Christ. He is not an invisible God, He is real and He is here, working in our lives, wanting us to abandon our sin and come to Him.

We praise our Savior in this freedom and for picking us up out of the depths of our misery, our contempt, our sin. We praise Him for being the God of grace and mercy. We praise Him for being our Savior and our God.

Lord, you are my Savior and I praise you. I praise you to the heavens and pray that you continue to be the light I need in this darkness.

What kind of hope do you put in God?

Come Into My Home

"Jesus replied, 'If anyone loves me, he will obey my teaching. My Father will love him, and we will come to him and make our home with him'," (John 14:23 NIV)

It's obvious when God resides in a home. There's more love, more laughter, and more smiles in a family that loves the Lord. There are no signs of violence, vulgarity or offensive behavior. The air is light and calming, even in chaos. God lives here.
If we love God with our whole hearts and obey what His sent Jesus to teach us, we will be rewarded with the love of God himself. It is at this juncture in our lives that God and Jesus, along with the Holy Spirit, reside together in harmony within us. They take up residence in our hearts, in our lives and in our homes.

Everything we do, every choice we make, every turn we take is alongside God. When we live this way, our path is clearer, and our road is straighter. Our vision is firm because we've invited God into our lives.

God, make my home your home. Reside with me and my family and help us make every decision. Create in us the need to put you first in our lives.

Lord, our only wish is for you to feel at home in our home. We open our hearts and our doors and let you in to rule in our place.

Does God live in your home?

Eagerly Await the Lord

"With all my heart, I am waiting, LORD, for you! I trust your promises. I wait for you more eagerly than a soldier on guard duty waits for the dawn. Yes, I wait more eagerly than a soldier on guard duty waits for the dawn"
(Psalm 130:5-6 CEV)

When we were young, we eagerly awaited many milestones: our 10th birthday, our first day of middle school, our high school graduation, our 18th birthday.

We wait with anticipation for these days to come; we watch the days count down on a calendar. As the day finally approaches, our excitement is almost uncontainable. The day finally arrives and we bask in the joy we feel for the moment.

These are the same emotions we ought to feel as we anticipate the coming of the Lord. He has made a promise to us that He will not break. He has promised to come back for us and He will, in His time. We should be eagerly awaiting His return. We should be watching and waiting, always prepared for the moment. As eagerly as a soldier on duty waits for dawn to be relieved, so ought we await the day when heaven and earth will become one.

Dear Lord, I am waiting for you. You made a promise to us and I trust you with all my heart. I shall stand guard as a soldier stands guard waiting for the moment when you come to save the world.

Are you waiting for the Lord?

Contentment is Great Gain

"But godliness with contentment is great gain. For we brought nothing into the world, and we can take nothing out of it. But if we have food and clothing, we will be content with that." (1 Timothy 6:6-8 NIV)

We spend most of our adult lives trying to build up earthly treasures like cars, houses, careers, boats, stocks, bonds, 401k retirement plans, jewels, and annuities. The pursuit of these items eats up most of our days, weeks, months, and years. We work overtime to pay for the house we want to live in Sundays have become just another work day to add to our weekly paychecks.

The media consumes us with the desire for more. They perpetuate the insistence that we never have enough. Keeping up with the Jones' is the only avenue for success. Somehow, we have convinced ourselves that last year's fashions are unworthy of being called apparel this year. A car more than four years old is ancient and must be replaced with a new one. Mothers who stay home to raise their children are selfish and lazy, and should contribute more to the family.

Where did we go so wrong? When did earthly possessions become more important than the Godly upbringing of our children? We came into this world with nothing and we are leaving with nothing.

Food and clothing are all that we need to survive. God will give us the rest. Reclaiming our families, reclaiming our lives and our free time will lead us all back to His arms, where we will always be content.

Dear Father, help me be more content in you. I pray for strength as I strive daily to get closer to you and further away from the world. This world has nothing to offer me, but you have everything I need!

How will you strive to be closer to God and farther from the world?

Another Power of Prayer

"Pray Continually," (1 Thessalonians 5:17 NIV)

My husband just had to have an MRI. He's already had an ultrasound and a CT scan, but they want to get a better look at him, so they ordered an MRI. Having already been through the other two tests, he thought it'd be the same kind of thing. So, he was shocked when he got there and it was this tube, for lack of a better word, that they wanted to stuff him in after strapping him down on a board. Once they got him in the tube and he opened his eyes, realizing the top of the tub touched his nose, he began to have a panic attack.

Needless to say, the MRI was canceled for the day. It was rescheduled for three days later, in a different facility with a larger machine. This time, we were able to mildly sedate him so the process was a little more bearable. He asked that I come into the room with him, just to be there. Of course, I agreed. After waiting more than two hours to begin the test, I was terribly agitated and my mood was starting to affect my husband.

Now, there was only enough of the sedative for one of us...and I didn't get any. So I had to turn to the only other power I knew of - the power of prayer. Prayer has many powers. It is the way in which we talk to God. It is how we form our relationship with him. But today I needed to talk to God to calm me down.

From the moment he was laid on the table, until the test was finally over, I prayed without ceasing. I prayed for God to lay his hand on my husband and guide him through the test. I prayed God to wrap his arms around my husband as he lay in the tube, comforting him from all that he feared. I prayed big, heavy, cumbersome prayers. And guess what? I was the one who was comforted. I was the one who calmed down enough to get my husband through this test. God not only answered my prayer with a successful test by my husband, but he also saw my need and met it.

I find it amazing how God will not only answer our prayers, but also see past them to our own need. I stood in the gap for my husband, interceding on his behalf, and God met me there. How does anyone get through these times without calling upon the power of God? I would have fallen apart had He not been with us through this.

God, you know what we need and when we need it. All you require is that we ask for it in your name; that your will be done. Lord, we give our lives to you knowing that you are able to get us through anything. We trust you to always be there when we call.

Are you able to lay it at His feet?

Go

"Dear children, let us not love with words or tongue but with actions and in truth" (1 John 3:18 NIV)

We were called to "Go." We were not called to meet, plan, discuss, debate, fundraise, poll, mediate, consider, vote, veto or table.

We were called to "Go!"

The best laid plans are just thoughts on paper until someone executes the plan. The best plan to help those in need is nothing until someone actually goes out and helps someone else.
So pick something, anything that will help another in the name of Christ, and go do it!
Don't hesitate to obey Jesus and His Great Commission.

Someone is waiting on you...TODAY!

Lord, lead me and I will follow. Send me, and I will go! I trust you that you will send me where I am needed most so I can further your word.

Where will you "go" today?

Do You Believe This?

"Jesus said to her, I am the resurrection and the life. He who believes in me will live, even though he dies; and whoever lives and believes in me will never die. Do you believe this?" (John 11:25-26 NIV)

Yes! Yes, I believe this. Jesus is the Resurrection and the Life. I do believe this with all my heart.
Why? I believe this because I have been on the other side of the fence. I have played for the other team. I know what it feels like to live without the light of Jesus in my heart.

I did not come to know Jesus until I was in my early thirties; just a few years ago. I lived over 30 years of my life in the dark. I know how Satan deceives us into believing life is no big deal.

Satan is a sly operator. He doesn't have to work hard. All he has to do is plant doubt in our mind. This doubt is all it takes for the human mind to run amok. We do all the hard work ourselves. We destroy our bodies, our relationships, our marriages, and our careers all on our own. Satan simply plants the seed of doubt and moves on to his next victim.

Once I started living my life for Jesus, I saw an instant improvement. My thoughts were purer, my actions were more guided, my personality, my choices and my decisions were easier to make because I first made the decision to allow Jesus, and not Satan, to control my life. Yes, I believe this.

Lord, you are my Lord. You are my controller, my stronghold, my strength. Without you I am lost; without you I am nothing. Please stay in my life everyday and guide my every thought.

Do you believe this?

Soft, Gentle Whisper

"The LORD said, "Go out and stand on the mountain in the presence of the LORD, for the LORD is about to pass by." Then a great and powerful wind tore the mountains apart and shattered the rocks before the LORD, but the LORD was not in the wind.

After the wind there was an earthquake, but the LORD was not in the earthquake. After the earthquake came a fire, but the LORD was not in the fire. And after the fire came a gentle whisper." (1 Kings 19:11-12 NIV)

Sometimes, God smacks me up-side the head. There are times when what I did was so blatantly wrong that He's had to hand me one, right in the kisser.

But that is not always the case. Sometimes, God needs to "pass by" and we have to be looking for Him or we'll miss Him. It's not always the earthquake or the fire; sometimes it's the gentle whisper.
If we think about if for a minute, God could show Himself anytime He chose. He could light the burning bush and say, HEY! Look over here!"

There are many times throughout the Bible where such interactions took place.

Sometimes, though, God wants us to search for Him. He wants us to understand for ourselves that we need to actively seek His presence. These are the times we can find him in the gentle whisper. And how glorious is it when we realize that He's been there all along, quietly, gently speaking to us as a lover might speak to his beloved. I have found that the times I realize God is gently holding me are some of the strongest, most profound moments of my faith.

Abba, hold me. Let me actively seek your gentle voice so that I know you are always here. I trust you enough to not always need to boldly hear you.

Are you quiet long enough to hear God whispering to you?

Sun and Stars

"You own the day, you own the night; you put stars and sun in place. You laid out the four corners of earth, shaped the seasons of summer and winter." (Psalm 74:17 The Message)

Sometimes, we need to praise God for who he is. A clear crisp night when the starts are visible is a perfect example. Spend some time gazing at the stars. Feel infinitesimal; it's good for the soul.

Our culture requires that we believe we are the most important creature on the earth. Spending time pondering the vastness of the galaxy should put our pride in check. Consider the fact that God simply spoke the universe into being.

He spoke the words and it existed. Billions of stars are in the sky. Is it possible that God put that many stars in the sky just so we could stand in awe and realize how small we really are? Could the nighttime sky be our reality check?

What about the beauty of the seasons? The earth rotates perfectly so that the seasons affect the land in such a way as to give the correct balance of light, water, wind and sun for the crops to grow. The cycle is repeated all but perfectly each year.

The ground contains the perfect amount of nutrients needed to blossom life from a seed and to continue that life through harvest. The minute atoms necessary to place all of this in motion were long ago contemplated and brought to fruition by our Maker.

Lord, the enormity of all that you created should be all we need to know that we are yours and yours alone. Keep me humble. If I should ever consider myself higher than a mere human, Lord I pray that you will put me back in my place.

Doesn't it feel good to be small?

Every Good Work

"God is able to make all grace abound to you, so that in all things at all times, having all you need, you will abound in every good work"   (2 Corinthians 9:8 NIV)

Have you ever noticed that when you are doing God's will, nothing can stop you? If you are performing works as God has led you and you can feel that in your heart, you know you will succeed; God will see to it.

God has this amazing ability to 'clear the path' for us. Whatever it is that we are doing in His name, as long as it is in accordance with His will, He will forge ahead of us, clearing the path for our arrival, much like a scout in the military.

He will make sure we have what we need to accomplish His task. God delights when we walk His path and do His works. He blesses us with His grace and His hand in everything we do.

Lord, what I do I do for You. Stand by me as I make this journey on your behalf. Help me attain the goals you have set for me.

What will you do with the path God has cleared for you?

Gifts

"Each one should use whatever gift he has received to serve others, faithfully administering God's grace in its various forms" (1 Peter 4:10 NIV)

Every single one of us is given a spiritual gift when we become baptized by the Holy Spirit. We are given these gifts so that we may use them in faithful servitude of the gospel. We won't use our gifts because we have to, we'll use them because we want to. We'll use our gifts because the Holy Spirit will have left a fire in our hearts alongside our gift, so that we have no choice but to rejoice in His name and do so with our gifts.

The more we use our gifts, the more skilled we become. When we work for the glory of God and not the glory of man, we flourish. Using the gifts that God gave us not only enhances our life with a new-found purpose, but clearly shows that God is in control and that we could never do the things we accomplish without Him.

Lord, work through me. Fire my gift and let it shine in me so bright that if I don't proclaim your glory, the very rocks will cry out. Let others see in me what you can do for them.

What are your gifts?

For the Glory of His Presence

"Praise the LORD for the glory of his name; worship the LORD because he is holy" (Psalm 29:2 NCV)

The worship set is usually my favorite part of church service. It is a time in my church when hundreds of people gather with the sole purpose of giving glory and honor to God, it is when we worship Him because He is holy. The lights dim, the music starts, I close my eyes and raise my hands.

I offer songs of praise to the Lord God Almighty. I sing! I cry! I stand in awe of God, I am awe struck at who He is and what He has done for me.

There is no other figure of authority that invokes these kinds of emotions. My boss, my city's mayor, not even the President of the United States can bring out those kinds of feelings in me. It is because the Maker of the entire universe cares enough about me to be a real, integral part of my everyday life. He loved me enough to send His son to die for my sins that I hadn't even made yet. This is the God I serve; this is the God who has my heart.

God, I praise you; I raise my hands to you giving you all the glory simply because you are God. I worship you for you are the holy one. Forever I shall lift my eyes to the heavens and praise your name.

Do you worship God? Really worship Him in spirit and in truth?

Continue

"So then, just as you received Christ Jesus as Lord, continue to live in him, rooted and built up in him, strengthened in the faith as you were taught, and overflowing with thankfulness." (Colossians 2:6-7 NIV)

It doesn't end when we get baptized. If we do it right, it's just beginning. He worked on us all our lives to get us to the point where we decided to come to Him. For us to accept him and then ignore the rest of the commands is an insult to God and an insult to salvation itself.

We are called to go, to do, to be, to learn, to serve, to give, to help. These are all actions. None of Jesus' sermons or teachings tells us to go to church and sit in a pew for one hour a week. No, brothers and sister – we are called to get our hands dirty.

We are not called to feed the hungry because they are hungry. We are not called to visit the sick because they are sick. We are called to do these things because in these actions we strengthen our faith. In these actions we find ourselves more thankful for what we do have and for whom we are.

So, if we are to grow in Christ, we must obey his teachings. We must serve the least of these, because it is when we do, that we serve Christ (Matthew 25:40).

Lord, give me the courage and the strength, through your grace, to do the actions you require of me. I want to be rooted in you; I want to love my life with overflowing thankfulness. Teach me how, Lord.

Is God showing you how to continue?

Make the Most of Today

"No one knows about that day or hour, not even the angels in heaven, nor the Son, but only the Father."
(Matthew 24:36 NIV)

If today was our last day on this planet, would we spend it in front of the TV? Would we spend it fighting with our spouse, our parents, our kids? Would we spend it staying late at work?

It is true, no one, not even the angels know the day and hour that Jesus will come back. Instead of living like we'll always have a tomorrow to repent and beg forgiveness, we should be living every day as if it's our last; as if at any moment Jesus will open up the skies and return to this earth to reign.

It's like the age-old saying, to live like you were dying. If we knew today was our last day on earth, we would live differently, love differently, act differently, work differently. We would be kinder to each other; we would hug our kids more; we would preach the gospel to anyone who would listen. When we know tomorrow's dawn will never come, we change what is important to us.

Make the most of today. Do something...anything. Why does it take knowing that today is our last day for us to do what we should be doing everyday? Maybe this is why the gospel is spread so much further in countries like China and India where preaching actually carries a death sentence. Evangelists in these countries are so effective because it literally is life and death.

So, step out...draw your line in the sand and decide that today is the day I will start to make the most of today...today I will begin to live like I am dying.

God, I pray that you would give me the courage to live like I was dying. I pray that you'd give me the peace to do the things that you are calling me to do.

How will you make the most of today?

Freedom

"For dear brothers, you have been given freedom: not freedom to do wrong, but freedom to love and serve each other" **(Galatians 5:13 TLB)**

An opposition to following Christ, even for some believers, is the inevitable accountability of resisting the sinful nature that we've become so accustomed to in this world. If we are serious, we know that once we declare Jesus as our Lord and Savior and become baptized, our life must change.

Some believe that giving up the sinful nature means to become imprisoned. I believe that is a trick of Satan. He makes us think that we will go without and be forever wanting if we turn from our sinful ways. It is as if Satan says to us, "Look at all the things you won't be able to do anymore."

This cannot be further from the truth. We come to the throne broken, asking to be made whole. Once we become believers, the Holy Spirit will then work in our lives to make us better people. We are given a freedom that cannot be contained, and it cannot be measured. Our freedom in Christ allows us to love and serve one another. No longer will our sinful nature be something we yearn for.

The satisfaction and peace in our hearts we receive from this freedom excels far beyond anything we had before.

Lord, you hold the keys. Free me from this life. Free me from my thoughts, my desires, and my weaknesses. Free me to become the steward you need me to be. Free my soul.

Do you feel the satisfaction of freedom?

Giving, Not Getting

"Don't pick on people, jump on their failures, criticize their faults— unless, of course, you want the same treatment. Don't condemn those who are down; that hardness can boomerang. Be easy on people; you'll find life a lot easier. Give away your life; you'll find life given back, but not merely given back—given back with bonus and blessing. Giving, not getting is the way. Generosity begets generosity." (Luke 6:37-38 The Message)

These are the ways we are supposed to live our lives, everyday. We would never want someone to pick on us, yet we are so quick to pick on others. The flaw that is causing the plank to be in our own eye is usually the flaw we see the easiest in others.

Like a good piece of common sense, we are told not to kick someone who is down, lest that hardness we show can boomerang back to our own lives. I believe that God puts people who are down on their luck directly in our paths to see what we will do.
Do we pay for a meal when a homeless and obviously hungry person stands near us in a food line? Do we offer a blanket to a single mom and child who are outside and cold? Did we walk right past the person crouched in the corner holding a cup begging for money as we jingle the change in our own pockets?

I don't believe in happenstance. I think random acts of kindness happen to those few people who step up and stand out in faith.

How can God give to us if we won't give to others? Why do we have to hold on to what we have so tightly, stepping over those who need so little, as we climb up society's ladder? Giving our lives and what we have, blesses us far more than any worldly possession can.

Lord, here I am. Take me and all that I have. Melt my heart; use me to show others how we should treat each other. I want to give to others as you have given to me.

How can you give to others?

God is My Salvation

"Surely God is my salvation; I will trust and not be afraid. The LORD, the LORD, is my strength and my song; he has become my salvation" (Isaiah 12:2 NIV)

Before I was a Christian, I felt I had to take on the world alone. I had to trust in myself to get through the hard times, and there were a lot of hard times. I felt the demons, they were all around, everywhere I turned, waiting for me to slip ever closer to the abyss.

But now that I am saved and Jesus resides in my heart along with the power of the Holy Spirit, I no longer have to live in fear. It took me a while to figure out what was so different after my baptism. Then, one day not long ago, I figured it out; the demons were gone. I realized that I no longer look over my shoulder; the thoughts of someone wandering close to me are gone, forever. God is my salvation and He is with me always, I have nothing to fear now.

I depend on God, I need Him for my strength and He is my song. I sing to my Lord every chance I get, praising His name; I glorify His son and the presence of the Holy Spirit in my soul. I feel it, just as I used to feel the demons. I know my God is with me, He is my salvation, I can feel it.

My God, you are my salvation, my light and my life. I know you are my strength and I sing my praises to you every day. Lord, stay in my life and keep me safe from the evils that lurk just beyond those that you protect.

Are you afraid?

Mustard Seed

"If you have faith as small as a mustard seed, you can say to this mountain, 'Move from here to there' and it will move. Nothing will be impossible for you." (Matthew 17:20 NIV)

Recently, I attended a wedding. It was a beautiful Christ-centered outside wedding. There was only one problem, it had rained all morning. Finally, around noon the rain ceased. A group of us prayed for wind to dry the grass. What happened next was unbelievable. As quickly as we prayed, the wind picked up and gale force winds dried the grass just in time for the wedding. This was the second time I had seen prayer answered instantly.
The first happened when my husband was on a medical mission trip in Haiti. A boy was dying on the operating table. The doctors rushed in and asked all the missionaries to pray. Within two days, the boy returned to his home on the mountain, fully recovered.

The power of prayer, for those who believe, can move mountains. When we boldly pray with faith, God hears us. He wants us to trust him, to believe in him, to need him. He wants to answer prayers that are prayed to him that only he can answer. All of this is done to glorify our Lord, the one who created all that we have.

Lord, I offer up my faith to you. I believe in you with everything I have. When I pray to you, I pray with thanksgiving, with love and with reverence. You are the one, the alpha and the omega. It is through you that we have everything.

Do you believe, in your heart, that you can move mountains?

Encourage Your Children

"Therefore encourage one another and build each other up, just as in fact you are doing." (1 Thessalonians 5:11 NIV)

You've seen them. Teens who've been told they're nothing. They walk around with their head down. Some of them look like they're mad at the world, living their lives with a scowl on their face.

They aren't children, they aren't adults. They can no longer be irresponsible, but they do not always possess the skills (physical or emotional) to be responsible. So, instead, they fall into some deep chasm in between child and adult that we call teen.

All too often, they are put down, degraded and embarrassed by the ones charged with nurturing and building them up. The worst blows to a child's ego come from their parents. Even if parents don't use the words worthless, nothing, stupid, or lazy, this is the meaning the teen will walk away with.

We need to lift our children up. I'm not saying we need to give them a false sense of security, praising them when they err; rather, we should encourage our children, show them the right way so they can make good choices later. We need to be in their lives for them to learn from us.

Parental stimulation is vital in a teen's life. If a teen has withdrawn, it is possible that they were pushed away one too many time and no longer seeks interaction.

Go to your children today and hug them, encourage them. Love them. If we pass nothing onto our children but our love for them and for the Lord, we have done our children well.

God, I need you. I need you to encourage me when the world kicks me. I need you to build me up when the world says I am worthless. I need you in my life, always.

How do you encourage your children?

Guard Me

"GOD guards you from every evil, he guards your very life. He guards you when you leave and when you return, he guards you now, he guards you always" (Psalm 121:7-8 NIV)

As young children, it was our parents' job to watch over us and protect us from all the dangers that are all around. They feed us; clothe us, keeping us warm in a home. They are there when we excel, watching us grow. They are there when we fall to pick us up. When we are scared, they encourage us and when we are too bold, they calm us down. Our parents keep us in line and build us up so we can soar on our own wings when it's time.

God is much like our earthly parents. He guards us from the evil that's at every turn. He watches over us as we walk through our daily lives. He painfully watches as we leave His side and wander away from Him, but He also knows when we come running back into His arms. Our Lord is our guard. He has guarded us since He created us, and He will continue to guard us until we return to Him in heaven.

Father, keep me close to you as my earthly parents did when I was a small child. Never let me out of your sight. I need you to be near me to keep watch and guard over me.

When do you feel God watching over you like a parent?

How Many Are Your Works

"How many are your works, O LORD! In wisdom you made them all; the earth is full of your creatures. There is the sea, vast and spacious, teeming with creatures beyond number — living things both large and small" (Psalm 104:24-25 NIV)

God made the earth and all the creatures in it. This is an undeniable truth. Just look at some of the creatures. Look at all the different colors of the birds in the sky, or the uniqueness of the fish in the coral reef. Stand in awe at the sheer magnificence of the enormous blue whale. Observe the social interaction of a den of lions, or a colony of ants.

Pure happenstance cannot account for the way in which every atom in this world depends on every other one. Daily, we should praise the Lord for His unbelievable imagination to be able to create such a world. We should think about this every time we try and change the world from the way God intended it to the way man wants it. The most unbelievable part is that He created all this for us. He made the mountains and the oceans and the meadows all for us to delight in.

Lord, when I look at all you've done, I stand in awe of you. The beauty of your glorious imagination is beyond words. I thank you and praise you every time I look out my window.

Look around you. What beauty do you see that comes from God?

Encourage One Another

"Therefore encourage one another and build one another up, just as you are doing" (1 Thessalonians 5:11 ESV)

When was the last time you saw two strangers encourage one another? We live in a culture where we need to climb the ladder at any cost. This exercise is no longer used exclusively in the corporate world. We have to be the best basketball player on our recreation team. We have to be the best at Monopoly. We have to have the best kids and live in the best house and have the best car. We trample on people along the way, every day.

Why can't we encourage one another to just keep going? Why do we always have to be the best? Why can't we just be? In the beginning, the early church of Thessalonica encouraged each other instead of fighting amongst themselves for status and position. Being a follower of Christ was good enough. We are all one body carved out of one God. We should strive to live as such.

Instead of stepping over someone to get ahead, we should offer our hand in assistance to those who fall behind. God would do it for us; He has done it for us.

Lord, sometimes it is so hard to see you because I am too busy trying to get ahead in my own life. Help me step back and remember to encourage others along the way. You were there for me; I can be there for another.

In what ways are you going to be there for someone else?

Heal our Land

"Praise be to the LORD, for he has heard my cry for mercy. The LORD is my strength and my shield; my heart trusts in him, and I am helped. My heart leaps for joy and I will give thanks to him in song" (Psalm 28:6-7 NIV)

Things go wrong. It happens. Even when we walk with God, sometimes we stumble, and sometimes we fall hard. It is when we turn our heads to God and cry for mercy, instead of becoming bitter and angry, that God sees our trust in Him and He reaches down to help us.

We need to get to the point in our spiritual lives where we fall on God instead of on ourselves or on other objects of this world. When we rely on God and we cry out to Him, relying on Him alone, He is pleased with us and we know it is God who helped us. When I reach for God with my cries of mercy and He answers me, my heart is filled with His presence as I turn my hands up to Him, praising Him in song and in thanks.

Lord, hear our cries; heal our land. We cannot do it without your touch. You are the only one who can save this world from itself. Lord, I know this because I know how you change my life. When I cry to you for mercy and you are there for me, my world is healed, and it is only by you. Lord, hear the cries of your people tonight and reach out to them in mercy.

Do you hear God when you fall and cry for mercy?

Establish Peace for Us

"Lord, you establish peace for us; all that we have accomplished you have done for us." (Isaiah 26:12 NIV)

Do you ever feel like you can't get ahead? Have you ever had the feeling of life completely engulfing who you are as you try to get ahead? I know I have. There was a time in my life when I insisted on doing everything myself. I forged ahead, head down, like a bull in a ring. I plowed through life trying to get the things everyone wants in life: a bigger house, a nicer car, more money at work, and respect from others. I constantly felt at battle with myself and with those around me. There was no peace in my heart or in my home.

Then I gave it all to God. I gave him my aspirations, my wants, needs and desires, and guess what? He pulled through for me; maybe not exactly the way I thought I wanted it, but He pulled through for me all the same. Sometimes the things I thought I wanted, really didn't matter that much to the plan that God has laid out for me. I had to understand that it all comes from His hand anyway. I need to realize that all I have is given to me by God and his grace. So naturally, when I hand it over to Him to run my life, I am at peace because we are no longer working at odds. Once I understood that all I have comes from Him anyway. My heart was far more peaceful with the decisions I began to make.

Lord, everything I have comes from your gracious hand. Be with me and guide me through this life so that I may come beside you in the next. Bring peace to my heart and my home as I allow you to make the decisions for me.

Are you letting God lead?

Humble Yourselves

"Humble yourselves, therefore, under God's mighty hand, that he may lift you up in due time. Cast all your anxiety on him because he cares for you." (1 Peter 5:6-7 NIV)

There was a time when I would insist on doing things my way. I always knew better, or so I thought. I would fumble through life, stumbling on every pebble along the way, insistent that I could go it alone. There were people along the way that stopped and told me I didn't have to do this all by myself, God was there and wanted me to be a part of His life. All I had to do was accept Him and humble myself.

Humble myself? I was too proud, too independent, and too successful to need something as intangible as God. More importantly, to humble myself would mean that all those years I fought so hard to be a strong, independent American woman would have been for nothing. There was no way I was going to allow myself to fall into that trap.

Then I let Him into my life and instantly I knew that I was wrong all those years. Letting go and humbling yourself takes strength, courage and determination to allow God to direct your life. I wasn't turning my back on my independence; I was fortifying it with God's word.

To let God live through me allowed me to blossom beyond my imagination. No longer did I have to bear the weight of this mighty world alone. I have the Lord of everything by my side. There is no anxiety or nervousness about my next step. God will deliver me because He loves me and I trust Him.

God, you are my light and my world. You are the reason I am here and the reason I breathe another breath. I humble myself and give my will to you.

How long have you done things your way? Are you ready for His way?

I Will Delight in your Decrees

**"I will delight in your decrees and not forget Your word."
(Psalm 119:16 NLT)**

Children long for structure. Even the most misbehaved child usually conforms when confronted with an adult that consistently enforces boundaries. If a child's boundaries are well defined, their behavior improves as does their school work and social interactions.

We are all like children longing for structure. When we choose to not forget God's Word, and consciously live within the parameters of the bible, our lives are blessed and we live more productive, peaceful lives. We often say that we are winging it through life, hoping to make the right choices, but the truth is that God gave us the manual on life. He wrote the book and gave it to us so we could know where "out of bounds" really is. There is no reason for any of us to not know where the limits of acceptable behavior lie.

When we read His word and live it, we delight in His decrees. There may be parts I don't understand, and it will take a lifetime of study for me to get to the bottom of the harder areas of the bible, but there is one point I know for sure: when I live as God intended, I am always rewarded. My God delights in the obedience I offer Him.

Dear Lord, your decrees and your ways are perfect in every way. You are the Lord over everything, including my will. Teach me to always live my life in accordance with your word so that I may delight in your pleasure.

How do you delight in the decrees of the Lord?

Gracious

**"Let your conversation be gracious and attractive so that you will have the right response for everyone"
(Colossians 4:6 NLT)**

We are called to spread the word of Jesus Christ. Sometimes it's to people who truly want to hear the Good News and accept Jesus as their Savior. That isn't always the case though. We've all been there with that person who asks all the questions, trying to see how much we know, hoping we'll get something wrong so they can make their argument that their life is better than ours.

Therefore, no matter the person asking the questions, we need our words to be compassionate, loving and gracious. We need to proclaim the Good News accurately, as it is written. It is not up to us to inject our opinions into the bible; only to convey it. Our words also need to be firm and strong in the fact that Jesus Christ is our savior and that through Him is the only way we can have eternal salvation.

Along with our words though, our actions must speak for us. Our words are only as good as the way we live our lives. Those who are not believers are watching us, waiting for us to fall. We must live what we say or do not speak at all.

Father, I will do my best to spread your word throughout the land. I will do so with my words and with my actions. Let those who are watching see you through my life.

What conversations do you have with others?

Love Your Enemies

"But I tell you: Love your enemies and pray for those who persecute you, that you may be sons of your Father in heaven. He causes his sun to rise on the evil and the good, and sends rain on the righteous and the unrighteous" (Matthew 5:44-45 NIV)

God eagerly waited for each of our decisions to follow Him. He waited for us even when we turned our back on Him. He never gave up hope on us. Therefore, we cannot restrict our prayers or blessings and salvation on only those whom we love.

We must also pray these prayers for our enemies. It is only because God didn't give up on us that we were saved. It is no different for our enemy.

God allows the sun to rise even on the evil. Why? I think it's so they can witness the magnificence that is God. He sends rain to the deserving and non-deserving alike. For without these examples, evil would never experience compassion. We, as Christ followers, are to extend our hand to all, even those persecuting us. We've all been someone's enemy at some point in our lives. Imagine if everyone prayed for their enemies as Jesus prayed for His.

Jesus, you are the example of how we should all live our lives. You came to show us how to do it, yet we find it so hard to let go of our petty differences. Give me the strength and the courage to pray for my enemies as I would pray for my loved ones.

Can you love your enemies as Jesus commanded?

Make My Steps Firm

"If the LORD delights in a man's way, he makes his steps firm; though he stumble, he will not fall, for the LORD upholds him with his hand." **(Psalm 37:23-24 NIV)**

We see it every day, people, who for whatever reason, make a mistake or series of mistakes that leads them down a path so low and into such despair that it's almost no wonder they sometimes never find their way out of the darkness. When they keep falling, we think to ourselves, 'where is the bottom for them?' Watching their pain and sorrow is almost unimaginable for us.

To those of us who are believers in Christ though, He holds us by the hand as we stumble. We will make mistakes, and we will fall, but He will be there for us, beside us as we climb our way out. We will never be alone and we will never be in the darkness. Even through the worst of our times, we can be assured of the fact that our Lord will never leave our side.

But when we delight Him; oh what a glorious thought. He makes our steps firm when He approves of what we are doing. There is an old saying that I use often when describing ministry work, 'If it is of man, it will fail; if it is of God, it will succeed.' We know instantly when we step out in faith if it is of man or God. When it is of God and we succeed, it is a magnificent moment of glory for our Lord. We have the opportunity at that point to give Him all the praise for what has been accomplished.

Lord, I pray that you delight in the things I do in your name. I pray that you will make my steps firm and unshakable as I stand for you in my life. And Lord, when I stumble, because I will stumble, I pray that you will be by my side as I work my way out.

What do you do that is of God and not man?

New Heart

**"And I will give you a new heart with new and right desires, and I will put a new spirit in you. I will take out your stony heart of sin and give you a new, obedient heart"
(Ezekiel 36:26 NLT)**

Remember if you will, for just a moment, your old ways. Remember the old desires and old habits that led you far from the light of God. Remember the feelings of isolation and emptiness.

Remember how you felt about topics such as faith and God.

Now, recall the way you feel now. When we gave our heart to God, He took our stony heart of sin and gave us a new, obedient heart with right desires. We no longer yearn for our old days and habits. All of those longings and desires have fled from us. We look to make a difference in the world now. We strive to bring others to the light that is Christ. God has blessed us with a pure heart and He wants us to fill it with love and compassion, instead of the darkness that filled our old heart.

We have been given the chance to start over.

Lord, you have given me new life. You have taken this broken, empty person and filled me with a new heart, a new spirit. I will take this second chance you have given me and fill my new heart with love and compassion. I will seek the light that is you in everything I do.

What old desires has God taken from you?

Your Promise Preserves my Life

"Remember your word to your servant, for you have given me hope. My comfort in my suffering is this: Your promise preserves my life"   (Psalm 119:49-50 NIV)

I think one of the hardest topics for non-believers to grasp is a Christian's lack of interest of things of this world. I often get asked why I don't strive for the big house, why don't I want a fancy car, or my favorite, why we give so much money to the church. Lately though, I've taken a different approach with my illness. I had been trying so hard to be cured, that much of my energy was centralized around new treatment regiments. Then, the last trial made me so sick that I felt worse with the medicine than without it. Now that just doesn't make sense.

My body won't always hurt this bad. My heavenly body will be perfect. I truly believe that I will go through these trials in this world but there will be no pain in the next. I put my trust and my hope in His word. While my suffering may hinder my life on earth, His promise will get me through to the next, heavenly world.

My Lord, I trust you. I trust you with my very life. You comfort me just by being near. I live for your promise of Life.

How do you trust the Lord with your life?

You Are the Light in the Darkness

"Arise, shine, for your light has come and the glory of the Lord rises upon you. See, darkness covers the earth and thick darkness is over the peoples, but the Lord rises upon you and His glory appears over you," **(Isaiah 60:1-2 NIV)**

As Christians, we are called to be a light in the darkness. Those who are too weak or sick to be missionaries can still be beacons for the Word of God through their everyday lives. The phrase 'Missionary' doesn't just apply to those who go to Africa, Egypt, China or Haiti.

Missionaries are also the ones confined to a wheelchair talking to the nurses about the amazing things their God has done, or the person who reads the bible during their dialysis treatment and answers questions to patients nearby. There are so many ways for us to be the light over the thick darkness that covers the lost of this world.

These "local" missionaries have a harder time than those who travel hundreds or thousands of miles for a few weeks at a time. The local missionaries have to live their life on the mission field every day. Our existence is a battle being waged in the open for everyone to see.

Every pain is scrutinized, every setback watched for signs of weakness or backing down. It is so important that we live every moment knowing someone is waiting for us to fail. When we feel we can't go on, we have to praise God for the strength He has already given us and ask for Him to walk beside us when our yoke is too heavy.

Lord, be with me always. Walk beside me; hold my hand as I endure so that I may be a light for someone who so desperately needs to see you in their darkness.

Can you praise God through the hurt?

Why Am I Still Sick

"By faith in the name of Jesus, this man whom you see and know was made strong. It is Jesus' name and the faith that comes through him that has given this complete healing to him, as you can all see," (Acts 3:16 NIV)

There is no reason for me to be sick. I am a Christian. I read my bible every day, I live my life humbly and I am raising my children in a Christian environment. I'm doing everything "right." Why am I still sick?

I was given this answer last week. A good friend just found out he has cancer. He is an amazing, bold Christian, taking the Word everywhere he goes. I was so angry because there is no reason for God not to heal him...or is there?

I believe we are sick for one of two reasons. 1) so God can heal us and we praise Him, becoming witnesses to the fact that He is a merciful and powerful God; or 2) he doesn't heal us and we still praise Him and become instruments for His work. If we are sick, it's because we have work to do – in whatever condition we are in.

He put us here for a specific purpose, perhaps it's so we can be an inspiration to someone who desperately needs it. Maybe it's so we can lead a caregiver to Christ by our daily actions. God will work through us in whatever condition He puts us in. Sick or strong, if we work God's will, we will never fail.

God, work through me, in whatever condition I am in. If I am well, send me to the mountaintops. If I am sick, send someone to me who needs to know your love. Let your light shine through my life, even when it hurts.

Are you ready to let God use you wherever He needs you?

My Confidence

"This is the confidence we have in approaching God: that if we ask anything in accordance to his will, he hears us. And, if we know that he hears us – whatever we ask – we know that we have what we asked of him" (1 John 5:14-15 NIV)

Last year, I attended a prayer seminar. I knew I needed help with praying but I had no idea how they were going to fill an entire day with nothing but classes about praying.

This huge man stepped up onto the stage and began talking about the boldness of prayer and how if we ask anything that is in accordance with God's will, He hears us and it will be answered. He told us to pray as if it is already ours. Boldness in prayer; I had never thought of it that way.

From that moment on, my prayer life was never the same. I had a fire in the words I spoke that had never been there before. Living in the shadow of Christ allows us to go to the throne with pure hearts.

Heavenly Father, allow me to be bold in my prayers so long as my prayers are in accordance with your will. I approach you as my Father, and I trust that you will delight in the boldness I have for your name.

Are you ready to pray boldly?

Hard Days

""Does not man have hard service on earth? Are not his days like those of a hired man?" (Job 7:1 NIV)

Some days are harder than others; they just are.

There are some days you wish you never got out of bed...ever have one of those?

But with each dawn, so long as we open our eyes and breathe into the morning, we get the opportunity to try again. Sometimes, we'll have to take that day to make amends for what we did yesterday, or to mourn the loss of someone who won't be breathing into the morning. Sometimes, we'll even have several lousy days in a row.

It is important to keep in perspective the fact that we cannot change others...ever. We can only change our perception of others and our reaction to others. Sometimes, that is the difference between a good day and a bad day.

So, I challenge you today...draw your line in the sand and say today I will have a good day. Today, I will control my actions, reactions and my perceptions and look past the pettiness and into the person to find good qualities. Today, I will look past my own situation and find happiness in the big picture, or the little picture, or wherever you need to look to find peace.

God, I thank you for everything I have, even on the days I can't find anything to be happy about. You know my heart and you know that my temporary sorrow is just that, temporary.

Are you having a bad day?

It Takes Pain to Feel Joy

"Then I would still have this consolation— my joy in unrelenting pain— that I had not denied the words of the Holy One" (Job 6:10 NIV)

God gave me feelings. He gave me the ability to laugh, to exalt and to worship. He has made it so I can feel the touch of my child's hand on my cheek and He overfills my heart with love and joy.

It shouldn't surprise me then that He also allows my heart to be filled with sorrow and despair. Nor should anger or pain surprise me. How can I ask for only the good and none of the bad? For if I never know sorrow, how can I ever really know joy? Without anger, when will I know when I am truly at peace? If I never experienced pain, how could I possibly know the power of the soft touch of a baby's hand? Without exhaustion, I cannot appreciate when I feel so good I could soar above the mountains. God takes me to the depths of my misery so that I can feel the totality of joy and peace and know that it is by His hand.

Lord, it is so hard for me to accept the pain so that I can have the joy. But through the strength of your son, who is always with me, I strive daily to better live your will rather than mine.

Can you see the joy through the pain?

Give Me Strength

"He gives strength to the weary and increases the power of the weak" (Isaiah 40:29 NIV)

There are days I don't know how I get out of bed in the morning. I drag myself, hobbling to the bathroom and simply barrel my way through the day, just trying to get to a point where I can climb back in bed. I don't like days like that and they are becoming more frequent in my latest flare up. The interesting twist to this is that I am so busy; there is simply no time for me to be this tired. It's all Kingdom work, so it's hard to say, "No, I can't do this anymore."

It is during these times that I lean on my God the most, which is what He wants me to do anyway. When I can't do it all myself, I have to ask Him to help me. I have to stop and realize that there is a bigger purpose for everything, including how I feel. I get to a point where I just have to come before Him and submit my will. If I am to be strong today, He will make me strong and if I am to be weak today, he will allow me to be weak so that I may rest and reflect on His glory. God knows what's best for me.

Heavenly Father, thank you for the opportunity to live by your will. I know when I am strong it is only because you allow it of me. Your love and mercy are so apparent in my life. I pray that I will always submit to your will.

When do you lean on God?

Answer Me Quickly

"Answer me quickly, O LORD; my spirit fails. Do not hide your face from me or I will be like those who go down to the pit. Let the morning bring me word of your unfailing love, for I have put my trust in you. Show me the way I should go, for to you I lift up my soul" (Psalm 143:7-8 NIV)

There are days I just cannot handle life. The stress of the day is too intense for me to get through. I am edgy, unsure of myself, anxious and angry all at the same time. These are the days I need God's help the most. Even though nothing terrible has happened, my life feels like it is unraveling.

It is in times like these when I go to a quiet place and talk to God. This is when I am honest with Him. I can tell God exactly how I feel and what I need from Him to get through the night.

Sometimes, it's life's little things that get in the way. I find myself more consumed with the mundane distractions of life than with the big life or death decisions. I've learned that I need to boldly pray for those things that fall within God's will. So, I bow before Him and boldly pray for guidance, wisdom, and peace in my heart.

When I do this and fully trust Him, I find that by morning, I know which way to go and I know that it is by God's hand alone.

God, you are glorious and magnificent. I trust you to guide my life, everyday. I will boldly come to you and praise you for the wonder that you are and seek your involvement in my every moment.

How do you trust God in your everyday life?

Endurance

"I lift my eyes to the hills – where does my help come from? My help comes from the Lord; the maker of heaven and earth" (Psalm 121:1-2 NIV)

Endurance is something that is hard to come by if you are like me. Seldom do I have the endurance to finish a daunting task. The thought of pushing to the end is sometimes just too hard to bear.

Then I remember that my help comes from the Lord. He made the heavens and the earth; surely He can help with my little problems. He is masterfully at work, weaving all our lives together so that one person's life is touched by another at just the right moment. He has billions of these connections orchestrated together; forming the massive cohesion we call life. It looks like chaos to us, but I think God considers it endurance.

So the next time I can't figure out why I felt fine yesterday but can't get out of bed today,

I'll remember to endure; it's all part of His plan.

Lord, I want to endure, I want to make it to the finish line and have you smile upon me because I did your will. Give me the inner strength I need to endure without the exterior strength. In all things, let your will be done.

How does God help you endure?

You Have Done Marvelous Things

"O, Lord, you are my God; I will exalt you and praise your name, for in perfect faithfulness you have done marvelous things, things planned long ago" (Isaiah 25:1 NIV)

Sometimes I imagine life as one huge drama being played out on the stage we call life. I no longer believe in 'chance' or 'luck,' therefore, it must be design. While we still have free will, I do believe that our lives have been carefully and lovingly thought through by our Maker. I think God takes the time to inter-weave us into a pattern that will later make up the story of our lives. Our relationships, our milestones, even our failures are a masterful work of art spun by the creator of the universe.

God has a plan for all of us. Each one of us was made by God in His image. He made us because He wanted to; we are His design, His work of art.

God is faithful and He stands by us, even when we fall. He waits for us, eagerly anticipating that we make the right decision each time an opportunity presents itself. I will praise my God and His name, for it is only by Him that I am me.

Lord, you are the artist of life. Your creation is so beautiful, so well thought out. I stand in awe when I think of the landscapes you've created or the sea breezes you breathed into existence. God, the maker of all things, I exalt you every day of my life.

What marvelous things does God have planned for you?

Depths of the Grave

"Great is your love toward me; you have delivered me from the depths of the grave" (Psalm 86:13 NIV)

Our youngest son is my only biological child. The childbirth went so badly, I thought I was going to die. I know people say that from time to time, but I really thought it was the end. I was not saved, I didn't even know what it meant to be saved, and I believed I would die that afternoon without ever meeting the life that I brought into this world.

At one point, about 26 hours into a very difficult labor, my blood pressure dropped to a deadly 42/24. Bells and sirens went off, the doctors and nurses stopped trying to get the stuck baby out, and instead focused on saving my life. Almost ten years later, I can still remember the calm, surreal feeling of allowing death to come in the midst of absolute chaos. I remember telling my mother as they wheeled me past her and into an operating room that I was going to die and to please take care of the baby and let him know that I loved him.

When I think back on this moment, I realize that God pulled me back from the brink of death, even though I had accepted my death. He loved me enough and He knew that years later I would meet a man who would lead me to the Lord and my life, along with the life of my family, would become wholly devoted to Him. My God knew this about me and saved me so that I might later live for Him.

God, I am forever grateful for the second chance you gave me at my life. I will live this life for you and do your will in every step I take. You loved me enough to save me from the depths of the grave when I didn't even know your name.

Has God ever pulled you back from death just so you'd have more time to get your life right?

But Thanks Be to God

"But thanks be to God! He gives us the victory through our Lord Jesus Christ"   (1 Corinthians 15:57 NIV)

What else do we need to know? Our God loves us so much that He came down from His throne, became man, and took on the sins of the world. He died a death for all of us so that we may have the victory of heaven. How do we even get near that kind of love?

While there is no possibility of getting my feeble little mind around the wonder that is God, I often wonder why He bothered. I mean, if we are so bad, and we are so bad, why would He want to be near us? Why would He want us to share in the gloriousness of heaven if it is so apparent that we don't deserve it? Why does He offer us grace? We do nothing for it. Our acts are like filthy rags in His sight. He showed us the way time and time again. He has all but begged us to live as we should yet we don't. Why reward us with heaven? Sometimes I just don't understand.
And then, as if by chance, one of my kids will do something wrong, usually something that I have told them again and again not to do. What do I do? Do I throw the eldest out of the house? No. Do I condemn our middle child to a life of labor? No. Do I scold the youngest so badly that he'll have emotional scars forever? No. Why not? Because they are my children and I love them, despite their faults. I eagerly show them how to do what is right, even when they do wrong. I give them opportunity after opportunity to make the right choices, even when they don't.

I guess that's what God does with us. We are His children; He loves us no matter what. He will always be beside us, guiding us to do the right thing, even if we don't always take His advice.

Dear Father, how can I ever thank you for always being there for me? My precious Abba, teach me to live in your light all the days of my life.

Does God wait for you to make the right choices?

Ask and You Will Receive

"Until now you have not asked for anything in my name. Ask and you will receive, and your joy will be complete"
(John 16:24 NIV)

Being a Christ-follower takes a little practice, even for those who've been in church most of their lives. It takes time to develop the trust. We don't give our entire selves right away. We hold back until we understand that we are not going to fall. It takes practicing, studying, and meditating on the Word of God. Eventually, we learn to look to the Word before any other reference, but that does not happen automatically.

Much in the same way, as we begin our walk, we don't know what to ask God or how to ask Him. Our prayers often start out small and soft, and yes, even wimpy. We are afraid or embarrassed to go to God with our problems.

It takes a little time for us to develop the boldness to go to the throne. As the Holy Spirit works in our lives and in our hearts, we learn how to talk to God. We learn how to go to Him in the name of Jesus Christ with what we need.

Once we are aligned with God's will, there is nothing we cannot ask that will not be given to us. We have the right, the ability and the obligation as followers of Christ to bow at the foot of His throne and boldly pray for what is in accordance with His will.

Praying in the name of Jesus implies that we have given our whole selves to God. We are saying that we have decided to obey Him, and that we will allow Him to mold us. It's more than just a phrase to be muttered at the end of a prayer. It is actually a position we hold as surrendered Christians.

Lord, I come to you boldly to ask for your blessings and your guidance in my life. Stay near to me always so that I can easily hear your voice. Plainly show me your will so that I do not falter.

What will you boldly bring to God today?

Be Still

**"Be still and know that I am God"
(Psalm 46:10 NIV)**

If your day is anything like mine, stillness is a commodity. Getting the kids up and ready for school, doing the laundry, dishes, running from meeting to meeting, taking phone call after phone call; the chaos of daily life can be all-consuming. Add to that the intense and complete exhaustion that comes with a chronic illness and it's all I can do to get through the day. Amidst the daily buzz we put ourselves in, how often are will still so we can listen for God? I mean really still and quiet and just wait to hear from Him?

It's probably rarely if you are like me.

Luckily, we have a prayer room in our church where we can go and be still. I sit and listen for God when I cannot find quiet anywhere else. When my life gets so wrapped up in noise, chaos and confusion, God draws me to that quiet place where I can go and be near Him.
Sometimes, God purposely does not knock down the door to tell us what He wants; rather, we have to come to Him, on His terms. He wants us to turn everything else off and come to Him, empty. When I obey and come before Him, giving Him my full attention, I am never disappointed by His marvelous love and kindness.

"Teach me, and I will be quiet" (Job 6:24)

Lord, thank you for your gift of stillness. It is such a precious gift in my life. Thank you for allowing me the opportunity to come before you, placing my life on your thrown, giving my whole self to your will. I will be still and know you are God.

What do you hear when you are still?

Super Glue

"Haven't you read," he replied, "that at the beginning the Creator 'made them male and female,' and said, 'For this reason a man will leave his father and mother and be united to his wife, and the two will become one flesh'? So they are no longer two, but one. Therefore what God has joined together, let man not separate." (Matthew 19:4-6 NIV)

Imagine super gluing your hands together. Now, try to get them apart. Pull and tug and yank as hard as you can. Any luck? Now, get a sharp knife and try cutting them apart. Are you bleeding yet? Is the skin ripping away jagged pieces of your hand?

I think divorce hurts so badly because it is the physical and spiritual ripping apart of one person back into two. In the process of trying to separate the now conjoined unit back into two, both are destroyed.

God knew us so well before we ever knew ourselves. He created a way where two people are made into one and that one unit creates life for the next generation. It's a perfect and beautiful balance when it works correctly. That doesn't mean it will always be roses and champagne. No, rather, it is when two people actually work at staying together, through all the ups and downs that life brings. That is when that bond becomes stronger than super glue.

God, strengthen my marriage. Find my weaknesses and fortify it with your love. You are the glue that holds us together and together we will face whatever is put before us.

Do you know a marriage you could pray for today?

You are Forgiving and Good

"You are forgiving and good, O Lord, abounding in love to all who call to you." (Psalm 86:5 NIV)

Like a parent, God watches over us and He is forgiving and good. His love is what draws us into Him. All we have to do is call His name and He will answer. A good parent listens for the cry of their child and comes running when they call, 'Daddy.' Our God is the same way, waiting for us to call out to Him.

But we have to call.

If we humble ourselves and call His name he will answer with His grace and mercy. We must be proactive and seek Him. He is here waiting for us, but we must take that step in faith and reach out to Him. His arm will always be there outstretched and ready to take us in His arms.

God's love is immeasurable and He loves us in spite of our inability to live sinless lives. He loved us enough to give us His son and to allow that son to die for our sins. That is the ultimate act of love. Selfless, abundant, unconditional... that's my God.

Father, you are good. You love me when I praise you; you love me when I fall. You are there to lift me up and to carry me when I cannot bear the weight of the world. Teach me, Lord to have the selflessness for others that you continually show me.

What has God Forgiven you for?

Unfailing Love

"But I trust in your unfailing love; my heart rejoices in your salvation. I will sing to the LORD, for he has been good to me" (Psalm 13:5-6)

I love music. I love to listen to music and I love to sing. Praise and Worship music is very special to me as it sings to my soul. During service, the music starts and I raise my hands, offering praises to my Lord and Savior. I am filled with such love and peace for my Lord, that at that moment, nothing else matters but worshipping Him. My heart sings in the comfort that I am saved, I am loved and I am God's.

God's love for us is unfailing. It is forever. He loved us when He created us and He loves us today. For those who call Jesus "Lord," we can never fall from His grip. He holds onto us tightly. We are precious to Him, as He is precious to us.

My God, I will rejoice in you. My heart sings for you, my soul cries out to you in worship. Hear our cries, heal our hearts. Bring us closer to you.

How do you get closer to God?

Guide Me

"I will instruct you and teach you in the way you should go; I will counsel you and watch over you." (Psalm 32:8 NIV)

So often, we feel like we are roaming through this life alone; without direction or purpose. I think even some Christians feel this way. "If only I could learn the way I should go." I have heard this, even from within the church walls.
We do, however, have both instruction and direction; and both come from God.

Instruction comes from the Bible. If we only have one book, the Bible should be it. Within its cover is everything we need to know to live a full, happy and God-filled life. The keys are in the book. Living by it is the only way for us to live fulfilled lives. We were created to glorify God and unless we do, something will always be missing in our lives. We may try to fill the void with things of the world, but that will only lead to a larger, wider void.

Direction is provided by the Holy Spirit who dwells within us once we give our lives to Christ. It is the Holy Spirit, God's eye, who directs us in our day-to-day decision, motives and practices. The Holy Spirit guides us in the way we should go, moving us ever closer to that relationship with Christ that we are meant to have.

Lord, I give you my all. In return, I ask for your instruction and direction. Guide my thoughts, my heart, my motives, my decisions. Show me the way I should go and I will follow.

Who or what guides your life?

Treasures

"For where your treasure is, there your heart will be also" (Matthew 6:21 NIV)

Treasures come in many shapes and sizes. For some, treasures can be fast cars, careers, jewelry or money. These treasures can be dangerous because scripture tells us that where our treasure is, there is where our heart will also be.

When we treasure things of the world, our heart remains forever in the world. It becomes increasingly difficult to remove the heart from the world once it has laid treasures there.

Instead, we should treasure God, His son and His spirit. It is through these three that we have life, love and hope. Our hearts should belong to God so that we are not of this world. Keeping our focus on Jesus keeps our eye on the prize and allowing the spirit to work through us, transforming our desires to the treasures of heaven.

Lord, you are the giver of life, the maker of all. You are my treasure and you have my heart, always. Help me to keep you close so that I always see you and I never long for the temporary things of this world.

What do you treasure?

Love Comes From God

"Dear friends, let us love one another, for love comes from God. Everyone who loves has been born of God and knows God" (1 John 4:7 NIV)

Love - It seems like a simple word, we use it every day. In reality, it is one of the hardest words to define and to live out. What does it mean to love?

How is love really supposed to feel? I don't think the definition of love can be put into words. Instead, I think love is the way you feel when you see a baby smile at her mommy. Love is the tug on your heart as you watch lovers say goodbye at the airport gate. Love is the welling up inside as you helplessly watch your child struggle with an illness as you pray with all your might that the sickness be transferred to you instead.

God has called us to love one another because God is love. He is telling us not to keep these potent feelings only for our closest friends and family, but to share our feelings of love with everyone we come into contact with. God loves us in spite of ourselves. Why is it we can't love our fellow man regardless of circumstance?

God, show me how to love as you love. Guide my heart and soften it so that I may allow more people into it. Lord, I pray for love and blessings on all those who are against me in the hope that they will find you.

How does God love you?

Thank God for You

"We always thank God for all of you, mentioning you in our prayers. We continually remember before our God and Father your work produced by faith, your labor prompted by love, and your endurance inspired by hope in our Lord Jesus Christ" (1 Thessalonians 1:2-3 NIV)

As Christians, we don't perform good works for the accolades of man. We perform good works to spread the Good News of Jesus Christ. We also teach salvation to all those who will hear, until every soul has heard what God has done for us.

Having said that, we should always pray for our fellow Christians who are out there on the mission fields throughout the world, living the life Christ showed us how to live. We need to remember them as we pray to God for all the work they do. Their faith and their endurance is inspired by and continued through the love of Jesus Christ. Their lives are not easy; they are constantly threatened with persecution and punishment, simply for spreading the word of God.

These Christians need to be lifted up to the Lord constantly. Find the name of a missionary or another worker for the Kingdom and start praying for them, daily. When asked, most global missionaries say that our prayers, and not our money is what they need more than anything else.

Lord, you've sent these missionaries, these angels into my path. Lord, lift up these workers of your will. Place a hedge of protection over them and their families, so that they may continue to do your will throughout the world.

Which missionaries will you start praying for today?

Taste and See that the Lord is Good

"Taste and see that the LORD is good; blessed is the man who takes refuge in him" (Psalm 34:8 NIV)

Try it and you'll like it.

That might sound like a childish approach to salvation, but it's true. Taste and see that the Lord is good. We're so afraid to step out of society, to appear different; even if blending in means to continue in sin. If we take that step, and stand out in the crowd, everyone will know who we are and what we stand for.

For some, that is intimidating, too intimidating.

I implore you to step out. Break away from the crowd; remove yourself from the norm of society and do what they cannot – change.

The Lord will bless you and keep you. He will protect you and guide you; but not until you take that first leap of faith. Taste salvation, taste eternal heaven.

Taste the glory and wonder of the Holy Spirit.

Taste and see that the Lord is good.

Lord, I have tasted and I know that you are good. Take me in. I never want to go back to my old ways. Protect me; let me take refuge in you, for you are holy and good.

Can you step out?

Slow to Anger

"The LORD is gracious and compassionate; slow to anger and rich in love. The LORD is good to all; he has compassion on all he has made" (Psalm 145:8-9 NIV)

It takes a lot to make the God angry. A look through the Old Testament shows that it took continued disobedience to anger God. It took wonton disregard, by an entire people and the worshipping of idols for God's anger to rise to a level where He had to declare 'enough.'

On the other hand, God is quick to love. When we, as individuals, do something good in the sight of the Lord, we are blessed. He loves to love us. He delights when we do what He asks.

I believe that the reason the Lord is slow to anger and rich in love is because He has compassion for all He has made. God, as our father, wants us to excel. He lets us attempt to learn from our mistakes. It is when we make a lifestyle decision to turn from Him that His anger becomes evident in our life.

Lord, thank you for being gracious and compassionate. Thank you for being slow to anger and quick to love. Lord, you are good to me; therefore I will be good to you.

How has God been slow to anger in your life?

Praise Be to My Rock

"The LORD lives! Praise be to my Rock! Exalted be God, the Rock, my Savior!" (2 Samuel 22:47 NIV)

God is compared to a rock all throughout the Bible. Rocks are strong, unmovable structures. Mountains are made of rocks. Putting your life, faith and eternal salvation in something that we compare to a rock means that you know it is unwavering, unchanging, and undeniable.

Foundational beliefs cannot be swayed by personal objections, political bullying or government leaders.

Rocks are not broken easily, and when they are broken, they are still rocks, albeit smaller rocks. Their molecular composition does not change when you break the rock into smaller rocks. The rocks simply spread out and cover more ground.

I put my salvation on the shoulders of my rock, my Lord Jesus Christ. It is only through my rock that I am redeemed and have eternal salvation. I exalt my Rock, my God, my Lord, and my Savior.

He is, He was and He will always be. There is no other, I will praise Him all the days of my life.

Lord, I praise you. I exalt you for who you are, no matter what I am. You are my rock, you are my Savior and I will forever praise your wonders.

How is God your rock?

Plans Change

"But the Lord's plans stand firm forever; his intentions can never be shaken." (Psalm 33:11 NLT)

Plans change. Weekend plans change, business plans change, party plans change. We are a society that has learned that change is inevitable. We've been taught over the years to be flexible and to 'go with the flow.'

This thinking has led us as a society in a downward spiral. The standards we once held ourselves to as a people have steadily declined throughout the years. We no longer view the family as an inseparable unit. While this country was founded on Christian principals, we are no longer a Christian country. We now live in a country where the Ten Commandments are being stripped from our nation's courtrooms one at a time.

God's plans, on the other hand, do not change. His word is eternal. His thoughts and actions are without error. His intentions are clear and his requirements of us have never changed. We will never have to worry about God changing His mind on how we are to live our lives, never changing how He feels about sin. On these principals, we can build our lives.

Lord, your plans are firm in my life and I understand your intentions. Stay by my side as I walk through life. Guide me so that I may accomplish what your plan has in store for me.

How have your plans changed?

God Has a Plan

"In the past I deliberately uprooted and tore down this nation. I overthrew it, destroyed it, and brought disaster upon it. But in the future I will just as deliberately plant it and build it up. I, the Lord, have spoken!"
(Jeremiah 31:28 NTL)

Have you ever been struck down so hard, you were sure it was God's doing? He's done it before....Noah, Sodom and Gomorrah, Babel; why not us?

Maybe it is God; maybe, just as he did with Judah, he deliberately uproots us, overthrowing us, destroying us, bringing disaster upon us. Perhaps he has a plan.

God destroyed the world in Noah's time in preparation of building it back up to give us another chance. It makes perfect sense to me that he'd do the same with us. Maybe he's breaking me down so he can build me back up to be a stronger, fiercer warrior for him. Maybe he's preparing me (or someone who loves me) for something big down the road. All I can do is trust that he knows best.

God, I put my hope and trust in you knowing you have a plan for me and for this world. Give me peace as we go through this storm together, knowing the rainbow is not far behind.

What does God have planned for you?

No Divisions Among You

"I appeal to you, brothers, in the name of our Lord Jesus Christ, that all of you agree with one another so that there may be no divisions among you and that you may be perfectly united in mind and thought"
(1 Corinthians 1:10 NIV)

On the day of Pentecost, the Holy Spirit came down upon the apostles and others, and tongues of fire appeared above their heads. On that day, the church was born. It was not a Catholic Church or a Methodist Church or a Lutheran Church or any other 'named' church.

The church, the gathered believers of our Lord and Savior Jesus Christ, was born on this day. The minor differences that have cause division and doctrinal alienation were not to be part of the plan.

We are called to stay united as believers. If we fight amongst ourselves, how are we to effectively spread the word to those who need to hear it the most? Being united of mind and thought means that we are to behave as the apostles did after Pentecost, never keeping our eyes off of Christ.

Imagine, if all the Christian denominations stopped condemning each other to eternal hell and instead spent that time striving for the worldwide spread of the Good News of Jesus Christ - what would our world look like today?

Lord, I pray today that you soften my heart to all believers of your name. Remove all divisions from my heart and allow me to fully embrace take hold of what the church as meant to be.

How are you a united Christ follower?

Follow Me

"Follow me!" (John 21:19 NIV)

No! I don't want to. It hurts too badly. I have a hard enough time chasing my kids around, cleaning the house and working. I have no strength left by the end of the day. How am I supposed to get up and follow you?
No. I can't. What? You want me to go on a mission trip? Absolutely not! I can't, I don't have the stamina or the endurance for such a trip. We canceled our vacation this year because of how tired I always am.

Yes, I know I can trust you. Yes, I know you know how hard it is for me to get out of bed every morning. And yes, you are correct; you are always there when I need you. But, but... oh, alright Lord. You know what's best for me.

You've never given me anything I cannot endure. Yes, I know you've always walked beside me and carried my burden for me. Yes Lord, I will follow you.

If you are like me, sometimes, you just can't believe that God would put something that hard onto your heart. You're sure there is no way you could ever begin, let along accomplish such a task. When Jesus asked us to follow Him, He knew it would be hard, just as He knew what He was asking of Peter. Jesus knew that following Him would lead Peter to his death. Yet Peter had faith and trusted Jesus with everything, even his very life.

We have to trust our Lord, close our eyes and follow Him. He will never lead us on the wrong path. I have never been disappointed in any outcome that I let Jesus totally control.

Lord, you will never lead me astray. I am your sheep, you are my Shepherd. Lead me, and I will follow. I know you will be with me every step of the way and I trust you no matter what.

Where is God leading you?

All for Me

"Praise be to the God and Father of our Lord Jesus Christ! In his great mercy he has given us new birth into a living hope through the resurrection of Jesus Christ from the dead."   (1 Peter 1:3 NIV)

Of all the things God could have given us, he gave us hope. He could have given us any other attribute so we could finish this race we call life on our own terms, but instead he gave us hope.

The part that amazes me the most is that he didn't give us any old run-of-the-mill hope. No, he gave us everlasting life, come live with me in Heaven forever hope. He gave us life through death; his son's death; his death.

In his mercy, or his love for us, he came down from Heaven, became man and died all of our deaths so that we didn't have to pay the price he demanded in return for everlasting life. He loves us that much. He loves us as a parent loves a child; ready and willing to take the brunt of the pain on our behalf.
What then is this pain I feel now? It's nothing; nothing compared to the pain I should feel had God left me to fend for myself in this miserable world. I can deal with this small inconvenience if I get to spend the rest of forever with the one who loved me enough to die for me.

Dear LORD, my God, how you love me. You offered your life on that cross for me before I had the chance to sin. You paid the price for my soul before I ever placed a foot on this earth. I will forever be yours.

Can you endure the pain for just a little while longer?

This Isn't Supposed to Be Easy

"For the word of God is living and active. Sharper than any double-edged sword, it penetrates even to dividing soul and spirit, joints and marrow; it judges the thoughts and attitudes of the heart." (Hebrews 4:12 NIV)

This isn't supposed to be easy. No one said that living our lives for Christ was going to be a simple task. It takes blood sweat and tears to win a war; and we are at war. Satan is on to us and he lies in wait, ready to strike when he senses us starting to fall. When it hurts, we need to take a deep breath, call on Christ to get us through and persevere to the next moment.

God will use whatever we have available for his glory. If what we have is sickness and pain; He'll use it to shine through us. He may shine mercy and compassion; He may shine endurance and strength. We need to stand strong so that God can shine through us, through our pain and through our suffering. We are to be beacons of light; a light that shines back to Jesus.

Sometimes He'll call on us to make tough calls; difficult choices in a world known for taking the easy way out. God can and will use us to show the world what He can do. We just have to be strong enough to let Him. He may put people in our path that need to see how we act and react to the hand we've been dealt. God may choose to use us as he did Job; as an example of faith. We should always speak and act as though we are on trial.

God, use me. I am here and I am yours. Take whatever I have and use it to show the world who you are. I pray that I am strong enough to show the world who you are through my pain.

Does God use you to show the world what He can do?

His Love Endures Forever

"Give thanks to the LORD, for he is good. His love endures forever. Give thanks to the God of gods. His love endures forever. Give thanks to the Lord of lords: His love endures forever. To him who alone does great wonders, His love endures forever." (Psalm 136:1-4 NIV)

His love endures forever. Have you ever wondered why this statement is repeated so many times? There are 26 verses in this psalm and this phrase is repeated 26 times. I think a point is trying to be made.

No matter what he's done, or what he'll do; no matter what we've done, or what we'll do - His love will endure forever. It is before everything and after everything; it is in everything and on everything. His love is the centerpiece of our faith and our lives.

So then, if his love truly endures forever and his love is the cornerstone of everything; how could he have made us in so much pain and in so much sadness? The answer is that he couldn't have...........unless he had a plan and a reason for us to be like this.

I think God's enduring love includes the fact that we will sometimes suffer. Suffering is not evil; it can be, but not always. Job suffered. We found out that Job suffered because of his faithfulness to God. God was so pleased with Job that he allowed him to suffer for God's glory. God enduring love knew the Job would be faithful.

God, I am suffering. If you've given me the opportunity glorify you through this suffering I only ask that you give me the courage and the strength to do it well. I ask for the power of your enduring love to get me through this time.

Can you see that God's love endures forever?

When God Calls his Sheep

"and provide for those who grieve in Zion— to bestow on them a crown of beauty instead of ashes, the oil of gladness instead of mourning, and a garment of praise instead of a spirit of despair. They will be called oaks of righteousness, a planting of the LORD for the display of his splendor." (Isaiah 61:3 NIV)

Sometimes, the pain is too great, the disease has spread too far, the doctors have done all they can do. Sometimes it's OK to stop fighting. Sometimes it's OK to go home.

Sometimes God calls one of his sheep home. This is excruciatingly hard on those left behind. Family, children, friends; loved ones are all left to grieve; but we're also left to do so much more.

Even in death we celebrate life. Within the grief is the praise; within the ashes are memories; within the despair is hope - hope that we will be reunited. These sheep touched our lives for a reason; God had a purpose in even this.

In 2007, the Lord called Nattie home. She was young and beautiful; charming and witty. She loved her children and her friends. Diet cokes, bandanas and books sat among tiaras and purple nail polish. We were all blessed just to have known her. Those closest to her will never be the same, but in their grief there is joy.

Even when we lose someone, the joy of knowing them in the first place has to give us peace. The knowledge that we will be reunited with them gives us hope.

God, thank you for sharing your sheep with us. Thank you for every moment we were given. You are the Creator, and even though it seems too soon, I will not begin to try to understand why you call your children home so early.

Take a moment and remember the ones you've lost.

Only You

"May the favor of the Lord our God rest upon us; establish the work of our hands for us— yes, establish the work of our hands." (Psalm 90:17 NIV)

I will paraphrase what a dear friend told me not long ago....

"ONLY YOU can determine what your attitude will be every single day, and when YOU control that--huge changes start to happen. You are the one in control of your words, your actions, and your attitude. No one else."

We don't get to decide if we're sick or not. We don't get to choose which illness strikes us or what the severity of the symptoms will be. We cannot change time or further technology.

We can, however, control how we approach every day. We are absolutely in control of the manner in which we speak to others, think of ourselves and believe in our God. Attitude has a tremendous effect on the progress of any illness. Giving up, losing hope and falling into despair do not assist in recovery.
For some of us, God has made our sickness the work of our hands. What we do with this power makes all the difference in the world.

God, I am not well. I'm in pain and I am tired. These are things that I cannot change; but I can change the way I allow my sickness to affect me. Lord give me the strength to face every day with grace, hope and love. Help me share these feelings with the people I will come into contact with.

Are you ready to change your attitude?

The Bakery

"But thanks be to God, who always leads us in triumphal procession in Christ and through us spreads everywhere the fragrance of the knowledge of him. For we are to God the aroma of Christ among those who are being saved and those who are perishing." (2 Corinthians 2:14-15 NIV)

Imagine a city block. On one end of the block is a school teeming with the laughter of children at play. On the other end of the block is a row of abandoned houses, now only used as a drug den and shelter for the homeless.

In the middle of this block is a bakery. Every morning at precisely 8:00am, the cinnamon rolls come out of the oven. The entire block stops, albeit for just a moment, to take in the delightful aroma of baked cinnamon and sugar. For that brief moment, both the child and the addict share the same elation, the memory of home and their mother baking. For that moment, there is no pain, no drugs, no tests or bullies - there is only the captivating fragrance that fills the air.

As a child of Christ, God sees us as a fragrance; a fragrance flowing into the entire world, touching the saved and the lost alike. We belong to Christ; therefore God will lead us triumphantly, regardless of our limitations. Reaching out is what we are called to do and God sends us out, like a fragrance on the breeze, into a world desperate to know more.

God, I was made to serve you; use me to reach the world. Lord, I know that there are people out there who need to hear about you and need to love you. Put me into a position where they can smell your fragrant mist and beg me to tell them more.

Can you close your eyes and smell the bakery?

Living for You

"To the LORD I cry aloud, and he answers me from his holy hill. I lie down and sleep; I wake again, because the LORD sustains me." (Psalm 3:4-5 NIV)

Before I was saved, I spent days, months, even years trying to do things my way. It seemed though, no matter how hard I tried, nothing happened the way I planned. Inevitably, I made mistakes that cost me dearly. I never felt at peace and was always on edge. I always felt that I was swimming against the tide; that no matter what I did I would not; could not get what I wanted.

Then, the LORD came into my life and changed my heart. From that day forward, I was able to cry out and be heard. I felt Him hear me. I knew I was no longer swimming upstream in a losing battle. Before long, I learned that my life was his to begin with. Surrender is not giving up; it's freedom from the world and its binds.

Everything I do is for Him now. No matter the task, no matter the stakes, I work, live and breathe for God. When I do this, everything falls into place. Placing my life before God allows God to work in my life. I sleep because of Him; I wake because of Him; I am because of Him.

LORD, you are the ruler of the universe; you are the beginning and you are the ending. You were, you are and you will be. With all you have; you love me. For that; I am forever yours. Stay by my side so that I may always do well in the eyes of my LORD.

Do you live for God?

Strong and Courageous

"Do not let this Book of the Law depart from your mouth; meditate on it day and night, so that you may be careful to do everything written in it." (Joshua 1:8 NIV)

Strong and courageous. That's what God demanded of Joshua over and over during this time. Moses had just died and they were about to cross the Jordan River into the land that was promised to the Israelites. "Be strong and courageous. Do not be terrified or discouraged for, for the LORD your God will be with you wherever you go." (Joshua 1:9)

What was to keep them strong and courageous? The Book of the Law. The Israelites were to mediate day and night on the book, not allowing it to depart from their mouth. If they meditated on it every day, then they would be careful to do what was written in the book.

God calls us to do the same today as he told these Israelites thousands of years ago. 'Read my Book; learn my Book; live my Book.' If the Book is always at the forefront of our consciousness, we are more likely to live by it. If, however, we only open the pages no and again, when it suites our needs; we will never see its full blessings.

Therefore, I urge you to not just read the Book; live the Book. Take its pages and drink it in; allow it to work in your life. Allow the Book to change who you are and turn you into the person God designed you to be.

LORD, you are the author of Life; you are the author of the Book. As I open the bible today, I pray that you let the words work in my life. Show me that this Book is alive and that it is You.

Do you read the Word, every day?

God's Reset Button

**"Satisfy us in the morning with your unfailing love, that we may sing for joy and be glad all our days."
(Psalm 90:14 NIV)**

Just the fact that we wake up every morning should be a reason in itself to sing for joy and be glad all day at the wonder of God. Have you ever thought about what happens to our bodies when we fall asleep? It's truly remarkable.

Our heart rate slows, along with our breathing, and a completely different part of our brain takes over. Our brain and body work all night long to reverse what we did to it all day. All night, our skin toils to repair the damage from staying in the sun too long. It tries desperately to regain the elasticity that the sun pulls out of it.

Our brain runs through its checklist of "reset buttons" that it pushes all night long to "process" everything that happened during the day. This "process" sometimes comes through our consciousness as dreams, or nightmares if we'd been through something traumatic that day.

Our body does the best it can to create the optimum environment for us to awake the next morning feeling refreshed and ready to tackle the day. If you are like me though, my Fibromyalgia steals some of this away from me. My sleep is far from restorative because I am not able to fall into that deep REM sleep very long and it is this sleep that is needed to allow our body to heal itself.

The body is an amazing, wondrous work of art. God created all of this that we call "ourselves" and he was able to put us together in such a way that we could reverse some of the damage he no doubt knew we'd inflict on ourselves.

God, just the thought of my body and how it works makes me stand in awe of the things you can do. Instill in me a sense of pride when it comes to my body, so that I would endeavor to keep it as the temple you envisioned it to be. I should spend more time taking care of the body you have entrusted me with.

Words

I've been thinking a lot about words lately. A few weeks ago, Joe, our pastor, talked about a few words:

Perseverance
Courage
Forgiveness
Obedience
Love

His application was different, but the basic message is the same. It's important to ALWAYS live with these words at the forefront of your thoughts.

Perseverance - even when we think we can't...even when we think we've lost...we have to vigilantly push forward through this life with nothing but the hope of God for our tomorrow. He needs to be the reason we get up in the morning, the reason we go to work-school-whatever, the reason we do whatever it is we do....even when it's hard.

Courage - because it is going to be hard. Jesus never ever said it was going to be easy. He said we'd be persecuted, he said we'd face everything the rest of the world faces. He also said be steadfast in prayer and I will get you through anything.

Forgiveness - how can we expect to be forgiven, yet not forgive. If we hold on to old, rusty squabbles and bickering, we are missing out on the beautiful release forgiveness brings. Stop carrying that baggage and make amends. It will release a hold on you that you might not have even known was there. It doesn't matter that they don't deserve forgiveness; neither do you.

Obedience - give it all to Him...none of it is ours anyway. Let go and let God be in charge of your life. Live through him instead of pigeon-holing him into a little tiny spot on Sunday morning. You'll be amazed at what you can accomplish.

Love - it all has to be done in love. No one was ever won to Christ in a fight. No one was ever bullied into salvation. It just isn't done that way. Love your God, love your neighbor, love yourself. Love is the greatest of all the commandments Jesus himself told us.

It is the cornerstone of....well... everything.

So, together with me, draw your line in the sand and decide to live these words with me. When we live with these words at the beginning of our thoughts instead of the end, as an afterthought, we live better, we love better, we are better.

God, teach me to live my life the way you want me to live it; boldly for you. Help me understand these words better so I can be a better disciple for you.

What words trip you up?

I Can't Take it Much Longer

"What am I doing in the meantime, Lord? Hoping, that's what I'm doing—hoping You'll save me from a rebel life, save me from the contempt of dunces. I'll say no more, I'll shut my mouth, since you, Lord, are behind all this. But I can't take it much longer. When you put us through the fire to purge us from our sin, our dearest idols go up in smoke. Are we also nothing but smoke? (Psalm 39:7-11 The Message)

Oh my gosh!!! Have you ever felt like you could not take one more minute of the pain you are enduring; not one more moment of the suffering? I came across the psalm recently and was moved to tears by the phrase, "But I can't take it much longer. When you put us through the fire to purge us from our sin."

I was thinking about the word purge. Humans are the only animals on the planet that shed tears of emotion. I recently read that tears of emotion are filled with a toxin, a by-product of stress. This may be why many people report feeling better immediately after crying.

Have you ever purged your emotions? Lately, I have been crying a lot. I cannot recall one day in the last month that I have not shed tears of sorrow, pain, frustration, and even anger. As I think on it though, I'm realizing that perhaps I am purging; ridding my body of the stress that I just cannot hold onto any longer.

God is so amazing, so completely fulfilling that he even created a built-in escape hatch for us. Sometimes, we can be like a pressure cooker and fill ourselves with emotions and angers and other stressors until we're stuffed, pulling at the seams. God gave us that little release button, tears, to ease our suffering, to allow us to release some of the steam we've accumulated. He loved us enough to know before the first tear was ever shed, before the first fight was ever had, before the first pain was ever felt, that we'd need a way to release these emotions.

Go ahead, cry if you need to. God gave us the power to do so. We may feel like He is making us walk through the fire alone, but He is right there beside us, holding the tissue box in case we need it.

Lord, I am just in awe of how complete you truly are. You knew before I ever took a breath, that I would need a way to release these emotions that I cannot seem to put into words. Lord, you are my everything and I can never thank you enough.

When was the last time you had a good cry?

Guard Your Heart

Above all else, guard your heart, for it is the wellspring of life. (Proverbs 4:23 NIV)

What goes in is what comes out. Good fruit will be born from those who feed their heart with good things and rotten fruit will be born from those who feed on the evil things of this world. We will all bear fruit. WE WILL ALL BEAR FRUIT.

Will it be good fruit or rotten fruit?

I started thinking about all the things that we face every single day. As Christians, we still need to be in the world, because that's where the people are that we are called to disciple to. But while we are in the world, we cannot ever allow ourselves to become of the world.
Guard Your Heart

Some of the evils that can erode our heart come in seemingly innocuous forms.
It comes from:
What we do with our down-time
What we watch or read when we're relaxing
Where we go on the Internet
The kinds of things we think is OK but wouldn't bring up at church

It's about being honest and realizing that it's not OK to fill our hearts with garbage and expect beauty to then flow from that same heart. It's about WANTING to not poison the ones you love the most.

It's about faith, love, marriage, family, life. These are the things that matter.

Guard your heart and you will guard these very most special items. It's about drawing a line in the sand and saying,:

"NO, I will NOT go there."
"NO, I will NOT do that."

"NO, I will NOT put myself in a situation where I can be tempted."

and it's about saying:

"YES, my wife means more to me than that."
"YES, my children deserve better than this."
"YES, I believe in this."

God, help me guard my heart. I want to keep it pure. I believe in faith, love, marriage, family and life. Make these the most important things in my life.

Do you guard your heart?

When God Trusts us Enough

"Then the LORD said to Satan, "Have you considered my servant Job? There is no one on earth like him; he is blameless and upright, a man who fears God and shuns evil. And he still maintains his integrity, though you incited me against him to ruin him without any reason." (Job 2:3 NIV)

Have you ever thought that sometimes we have sickness and death backwards? As a dear friend battles cancer tonight, I look on his life and his testimony, and I realize that God can't trust this responsibility with just anyone.

Growing stronger in faith in the face of death takes a special person with a special anointing. We all have gifts that are placed on our hearts by the Holy Spirit, and I will be so bold as to suggest that sickness can be a gift if we accept it as such.

What if God trusts us enough to carry His word through our own suffering? What if He believes in my friend, or in me so strongly that He can trust me not to turn from Him as my body fails or as the pain sets in? What if God knew we were strong enough to be the bravest of soldiers?

If we look at our plight from this new, refreshing light, we realize that we have been given a responsibility, not a burden. We are trusted, not discarded; anointed, not afflicted. The word the sick and hurting carry is far more powerful that any of us can imagine. To see the light of God shine through the eyes of one with an illness will open eyes and soften hearts to hear and accept the word of God and the Good News of Jesus.

Lord, if I search my soul and put aside my earthly wants and desires, I will be able to humbly thank you for trusting me with this responsibility of illness. It is hard for me to understand and sometimes hard for me to accept, but accept I will for I am your soldier, and I will let you shine through me so that others can see the glorious reward that waits for me just outside this body.

Can God trust you enough?

Listen

**"The LORD called Samuel a third time, and Samuel got up and went to Eli and said, "Here I am; you called me." Then Eli realized that the LORD was calling the boy. So Eli told Samuel, "Go and lie down, and if he calls you, say, 'Speak, LORD, for your servant is listening.' "So Samuel went and lay down in his place. The LORD came and stood there, calling as at the other times, "Samuel! Samuel!" Then Samuel said, "Speak, for your servant is listening."
(1 Samuel 3:8-10 NIV)**

I like to theme my years; it helps me keep focus. Two years ago, it was "Be Still and Know that I AM GOD." Last year, it was "God's Timing is Perfect." This year, I thought my theme was "Listening" but I could not have been more wrong if I tried. For the last month or so, God has been putting "Listening" on my heart. I honestly thought that Listening was to be my theme for this year. ....God was telling <u>ME</u> to LISTEN....
  Shhhhhhh....listen my child.

Let's be honest, 2008 was not the best year for many of us and I am no exception. My husband was out of work for several months, I got scammed with the publishing of my book, there were many issues with my family, a few issues with my health....I was OVER 2008.

listen....

And then, I was FINALLY listening...and it was amazing. I've realized that I need to stop running away from the past that no longer haunts me. Jesus took all that garbage away when he cleansed me in his forgiveness...I have nothing to fear.

I spent 2008 furiously running after things. I have everything I need here. He gives me everything; provides for every need.

For some time, I have based my spiritual needs on what I can give to others. He said it's time to get back to what I need.

Then he gave it to me.....Recovery. 2009 will be a year for me to recover...recover from hurts, from pasts, from neglecting myself, from health issues, from family issues. 2009 will be a year for me to be totally His.

This theme feels right; it makes me a little nervous too. I don't know how to make "me" important. I guess that's why it's my theme. I always talk about drawing a line in the sand, I guess God did this time.

OK God, you've got my attention. I will work on being devoted to you this year and devoted to recovering from this past year. I'll need your help though. LORD, please stand right beside me every step of the way. It's the only way I'll be able to succeed.

Are you listening to what God is trying to tell you?

Rest

Then the LORD said to Moses, "How long will you refuse to keep my commands and my instructions? Bear in mind that the LORD has given you the Sabbath; that is why on the sixth day he gives you bread for two days. Everyone is to stay where he is on the seventh day; no one is to go out." So the people rested on the seventh day. (Exodus 16:28-30 NIV)

My grandmother was in the hospital for a week and I hardly left her side. She was admitted on Christmas night and all of her children were in different parts of the country visiting their grandchildren. From the hospital room, I learning a lot about rest. I need to constantly be reminded that life is not about running as fast as you can to the other side.

Sometimes we need to rest.

Rest comes in many forms. Sometimes, we need to rest our bodies, like my nana. Watching her rest, I see that she gets a little stronger every time she does take the time to rest. Not long ago, I was so sick; rest was all that I wanted. Rest builds our bodies back so we can continue to move forward.

Sometimes, we need to rest our minds from all the craziness going around. In December, we usually find ourselves running crazy and we want more than anything to be able to turn our brain off. For me, I had to return to work on top of trying to help nana, so I was depressed at the notion that there would be no more rest for me.

We're called to rest. God took the 7th day to rest and it's commanded as something we are to do. I often wonder lately if the way we run ourselves down now is not a direct result of our refusal to honor the Sabbath? It's an interesting question to ponder. I have all day to think about it.

GOD, you've commanded us to rest, as you have rested. It's not just a rest for the body or the mind, but it is for the soul as well. For when we rest, we are better able to concentrate on you and your love for us. It is in these times of rest that we are supposed to give ourselves over to the bountiful mercy that you bestow upon us every day.

Do you rest as we're commanded?

Just Beyond My Praise

"I will say of the LORD, He is my refuge and my fortress, my God, in whom I trust." (Psalm 91:2 NIV)

It's easy to praise God in the good times. It's easy to thank him for all that we have. But what do we do when times get tough? What do we say to God when things don't turn out the way we planned?

Sometimes, we don't feel God's presence through a hard time. Perhaps we are having trouble in our marriage, or we just got news from the doctor that isn't good. Whatever it is, we feel like he abandoned us in our time of need. We cry out to him asking, "Why, God, why me?" Yet the truth is, he is there, waiting for us just beyond our reach - waiting for us to make the first step. That first step is praise.

True obedience is being able to lift your hands in praise even when the news is bad, even when the marriage is failing, even when dark times envelope us. God is there waiting for us just beyond this praise to lift us up and carry us through our most desperate times. He just needs to know that we come, through the good and the bad, in sickness and in health.

God never said it was going to be easy. In fact, He said we'd be marked, targets for the world.

Bad times will come, but it is our reaction to those bad times that help define our faith, solidifying our love and commitment to the King of all kings and the Lord of all lords.

God, it's hard. It's hard to lift my hands in praise when I have the weight of the world on my shoulders. Times are tough, life is hard. But I trust you enough to get me through it. So I will obey. I will raise my hands and praise your Holy Name, for I love you and you are my God.

Are you able to raise your hands and praise Him, even when it's hard?

No Ifs Ands or Buts

"I tell you the truth, if you have faith as small as a mustard seed, you can say to this mountain, 'Move from here to there' and it will move. Nothing will be impossible for you." (Matthew 17:20 NIV)

We've all heard it said, "I believe in God, but..." or maybe it's, "I have faith, but..." and sometimes we even hear, "I'd believe if only..."

The problem is that we put human demands and restrictions on our faith at the onset instead of trusting and waiting to see just how big our God is. It doesn't take very much effort to believe; the signs are all there. If our eyes are open and our ears can hear Him, we will be able to believe. Faith, however, is something completely different.

Faith takes time, it takes patience and it takes work. Faith requires us, as believers, to lay down the things of this world like timing, health, power and money and instead allow Him to work through us. Faith means standing through the hard times; it means leaning on Him when we don't feel His presence. Faith means being the hold-out and raising our hands in a world certain they can get along without their God.

If we can move mountains with the faith of a mustard seed, imagine what could we accomplish with full-on, sold-out faith. Could we change the world? Could we change a life? Could we save a soul?

Faith begins just before the "ifs" and the "buts." Faith begins when we close our eyes to the world and open our hearts to our Lord. He will not let us down and His paths are always straight.

Lord, I want to have faith. I want to let go of this world that I cling so desperately to. Please show me. I will loosen my grip; but I need you to catch me. I trust you God; I want you to change my life.

Can you just believe?

Love

**"Because he loves me," says the LORD, "I will rescue him; I will protect him, for he acknowledges my name. He will call upon me, and I will answer him; I will be with him in trouble, I will deliver him and honor him."
(Psalm 91:14-15 NIV)**

Love. It's because we love Him. Love is what it takes for God to protect us and be with us when we are in trouble. Love.

The more time I spend thinking about love, the more I realize that love is the great equalizer. We seek it, we need it, we'll die for it. Love heals wounds, binds families, endures time. It starts wars, travels oceans and conquers kings. We cannot live without love and we find it hard to breath while in love. Love rights wrongs and saves the day. Love brings us to our knees the way nothing else can.

It is when we are on our knees, so completely in love with God that He stands beside us. He wants us to love Him, because He loves us in the same unconditional way we love our own children.

Abba, you are my father and I love you. I want you to love me the way I love my own children. I need you to protect me and stay with me through all my hard times. Father, I need you to be my father. I love you.

Do you really know what love is?

This is Just a Season

"See! The winter is past; the rains are over and gone. Flowers appear on the earth; the season of singing has come, the cooing of doves is heard in our land."
(Song of Solomon 2:11-12 NIV)

I believe that this sickness is just a season. While the pain I feel now is real and there is no mistaking the difficulties I face, I know that it will not always be this way and that there is a reason for all of it. God uses everything for His glory, even this wretched body of mine.

We will all suffer. It may be chronic or terminal illness, which can be painful or debilitating. For others, it may be the loss of a loved one or loss of a job. In any case, the despair we feel is real and sometimes all-encompassing. Believers must deal with suffering just like the rest of the world. But we have one advantage; we have hope.

For after winter comes spring; a time of life and renewal. God allowed us to serve him in suffering. Sometimes it is so we are prepared for what lies head. Whatever the case, God will be there with us; leading the way into the cool meadow grasses of spring.

God, this is just a season and while I feel this decrepit body falling apart; I know you have a purpose for it all. I will be your soldier and get through the battle so I can bask in the sunshine of spring by your side.

Do you know that this too shall pass?

An Undivided Heart

"Teach me your way, O LORD, and I will walk in your truth; give me an undivided heart, that I may fear your name." (Psalm 86:11 NIV)

Our pastor preached about this topic; an undivided heart. The premise was that if our heart is split in two, we are dead. If that is true in the physical realm, why wouldn't it be true in the spiritual realm.

Not wanting to do the things that we once did is the driving force behind repentance. God changes us. The indwelling of the Holy Spirit changes what matters to us; it changes the way we look at the world and the way we treat our neighbor.

Salvation carries with it a sense of accountability. Jeffrey Dahmer figured this out shortly before his death. One of the most notorious serial killers of all time was changed when God gave him an undivided heart; a heart that no longer desired the evil of the

world, but only the love of the father of the universe.

Once our hearts are whole and pleasing to the Lord, it is then easier to shun from evil, easier to make the right choices, because we WANT to, not because we HAVE to.

Adoni, give me an undivided heart. I am so tired of living half in the world and half in your light. I want to come fully, completely to you. Teach me how, O Lord and instill in me a fear of your name that will carry with me all the days of my life.

Is your heart divided?

All That I Am

"All that I am, praise the LORD; everything in me, praise his holy name. My whole being, praise the LORD and do not forget all his kindnesses" (Psalm 103:1-2 NCV)

Many of us want what other people have. We all know people with more money, nicer cars, and bigger houses. They may be prettier, or have a keener business sense. For some of us, it's not easy to struggle with the bills as we watch our neighbor flourish. But God has His reasons, and he has a purpose for you.

We need to get on our knees and praise the Lord for everything that we have, no matter how big or small. He made us exactly the way he wants us. He knows of our troubles and our heartaches. He has us all in each situation we are in for a specific reason. We need to praise our God for just allowing us to breathe one more day.

Lord, I praise you for me. I praise you for the opportunity to live one more day so that I can do your will one more time. You are kind, Lord; you see the flaws in me, yet you use them for your good.

Can you be happy with what you have?

www.ingramcontent.com/pod-product-compliance
Lightning Source LLC
Chambersburg PA
CBHW021019090426
42738CB00007B/830